REDress

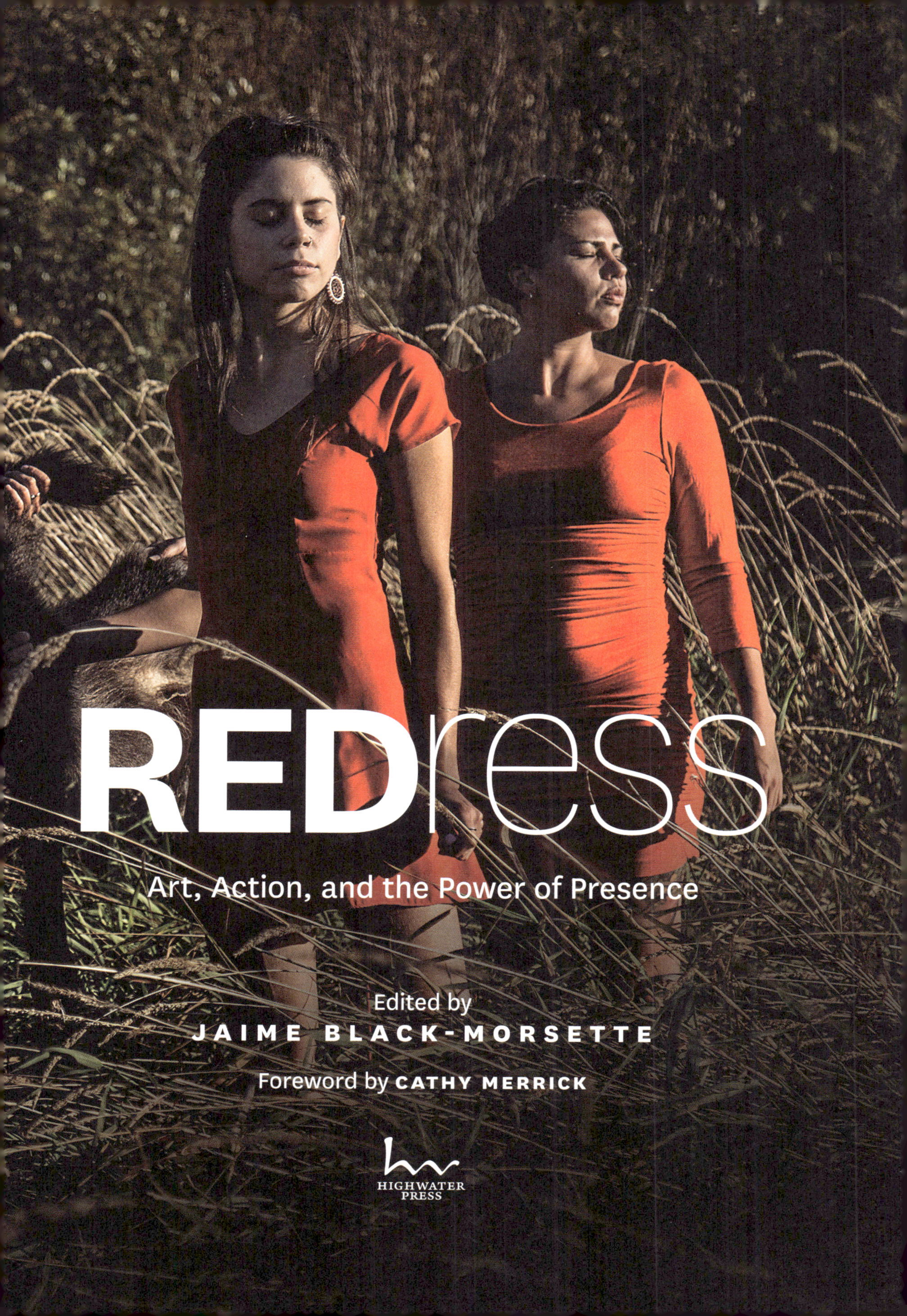

REDress

Art, Action, and the Power of Presence

Edited by
JAIME BLACK-MORSETTE

Foreword by **CATHY MERRICK**

HIGHWATER PRESS

HighWater Press gratefully acknowledges the financial support of the Government of Canada and Canada Council for the Arts as well as the Province of Manitoba through the Department of Sport, Culture, Heritage and Tourism and the Manitoba Book Publishing Tax Credit for our publishing activities.

Funded by the Government of Canada
Financé par le gouvernement du Canada
Canada
Canada Council for the Arts
Conseil des arts du Canada

HighWater Press is an imprint of Portage & Main Press.
Printed and bound in Canada by Friesens
Design by Jennifer Lum
Cover image by Jaime Black-Morsette
Special thanks to Aandeg Muldrew for translations.
Thank you to the student focus group from the MET Centre for Arts & Technology, Seven Oaks MET, and Maples MET (Winnipeg, MB) for their thoughtful feedback on the cover of this book.

Library and Archives Canada Cataloguing in Publication
Title: REDress : art, action, and the power of presence / edited by Jaime Black-Morsette ; foreword by Cathy Merrick.
Other titles: REDress (2025) Names: Black-Morsette, Jaime, editor.
Description: Includes bibliographical references.
Identifiers: Canadiana (print) 20240451740 | Canadiana (ebook) 20240451848
ISBN 9781774921388 (softcover) | ISBN 9781774921432 (EPUB) | ISBN 9781774921449 (PDF)
Subjects: LCSH: Indigenous women—Canada—Social conditions. | LCSH: Indigenous women—Crimes against—Canada. | LCSH: Indigenous women—Violence against—Canada. LCSH: Black-Morsette, Jaime. REDress project. | LCSH: Installations (Art)—Canada. LCSH: Political art—Canada. | LCSH: Social justice in art.
Classification: LCC E98.W8 R43 2025 | DDC 305.48971—dc23

28 27 26 25   1 2 3 4 5

This book is printed on FSC-certified paper made with 30% post-consumer waste using vegetable-based inks and alcohol-free blanket wash. It was printed in North America by Friesens, the first FSC-certified printing company in Canada. With plants powered by hydroelectric and wind farms, the company is 100% employee-owned and is committed to minimizing its ecological footprint.

FSC www.fsc.org
MIX
Paper | Supporting responsible forestry
FSC® C016245

ENVIRONMENTAL BENEFITS STATEMENT

Portage & Main Press saved the following resources by printing the pages of this book on chlorine free paper made with 30% post-consumer waste.

TREES	WATER	ENERGY	SOLID WASTE	GREENHOUSE GASES
29 FULLY GROWN	2,300 GALLONS	12 MILLION BTUs	100 POUNDS	12,300 POUNDS

Environmental impact estimates were made using the Environmental Paper Network Paper Calculator 4.0. For more information visit www.papercalculator.org

HIGHWATER PRESS
www.highwaterpress.com
Winnipeg, Manitoba
Treaty 1 Territory and homeland of the Métis Nation

Table of Contents

CONTENT WARNING

The content in these pages is a heavy bundle to carry. The works in this collection share first-hand accounts of the historical and ongoing colonial violence against Indigenous women, girls, and Two-Spirit people. Through the sharing of these stories, we are also invited to gather around the fire of resistance and the warmth of resilience conveyed in the words of the women, girls, and Two-Spirit people standing their ground against this violence and erasure. The weight of these words is meant for us all to carry together. For support and emotional assistance related to Missing and Murdered Indigenous Women and Girls call the Canadian toll-free 24/7 crisis line at 1-844-413-6649. If you are in crisis in Canada or the United States please call or text the Suicide Crisis Helpline at 988.

Foreword

CATHY MERRICK (1962–2024)

Cathy was a grandmother to us all, lifting us up while tirelessly standing her ground to defend what was right. For the two years before her passing Cathy stood on the frontlines and behind the scenes to support the efforts of Cambria Harris and the Search The Landfill movement. She went toe to toe against all opposition to the search, lending her powerful voice to every rally and gathering on the steps of the Manitoba Legislature. The last time I saw her we were at the Camp Morgan powwow celebrating the beginning of the search. — Jaime Black-Morsette

IN THE DEPTHS OF CANADA'S HISTORY lie chapters often overlooked, stories untold, and voices unheard. These are the stories of Indigenous women, girls, and Two-Spirit individuals who have been victims of a silent epidemic known as Missing and Murdered Indigenous Women, Girls, and Two-Spirit people (MMIWG2S). Each page of this book holds the marks of loss, while reminding us of love's ability to nurture a collective responsibility that perseveres against the luxury of indifference. Reading this book means taking on the responsibility to act upon its truths with the hope that one day our scars will heal, and Canada's national shame of MMIWG2S will be a distant memory.

The targeted victimization and exploitation of First Nations, Inuit, and Métis women is often referred to by governments and Canadians alike as a "crisis." However, when we speak about MMIWG2S we must carefully consider the words we use. The danger in labelling MMIWG2S as a crisis is the associated implication that the killing and abuse of Indigenous women has emerged as an unexpected, non-routine event—an implication that could not be further from the truth in this context. This is not a recent phenomenon nor a temporary blip in Canada's history. It is a long-standing genocide that haunts every intersection of Indigenous identity, integral to the history of Western expansion and the settling of what is now called Canada. The devastating loss of Indigenous life is not an isolated or sudden curiosity, but a pervasive, deliberate, and systemic issue buried in the foundation of this country.

It is within this context of historical and ongoing oppression that grassroots women have emerged as the vanguard of the struggle for justice. They are the mothers who refuse to let their daughters' disappearances go unnoticed, the sisters who demand accountability, the grandmothers who carry the weight of generational trauma yet still find the strength to fight. Their voices are the loudest, their actions the most resolute, and their resilience the most enduring.

The power of women in this movement cannot be overstated. It is in the tears they shed, the songs they sing, and the stories they tell that the true strength of Indigenous women shines through. They are the heart and soul of the MMIWG2S movement, driving it forward with unwavering determination and love. Their activism is not just about seeking justice for their own loved ones but about advocating for systemic change that will protect future generations.

At the heart of this movement stands the REDress Project, conceived by the visionary Métis artist Jaime Black-Morsette. Jaime's work transcends the boundaries of art and activism, creating a deeply moving and intimate representation of absence and loss. Jaime has brought the issue of MMIWG2S to the public consciousness, as red dresses have now emerged as a universal symbol of MMIWG2S. Whether hung along highways, on fences, or from trees, the red dress is now the silent witness that urges us to remember the people who should have worn them.

The choice of red for these dresses is significant. In many Indigenous cultures, red is believed to be the only colour that spirits can see. The dresses thus serve as a compass, calling back the spirits of those who have been lost, ensuring they are not forgotten. This visual representation is in and of itself a profound act of reclamation. By hanging these dresses, we are invited to confront the void they represent and to understand the depth of loss endured by Indigenous families, communities, and nations.

Awareness is the first step toward change, but it cannot be the last. The works shared in this book underscore the necessity of moving from awareness to action. This means advocating for policy changes, supporting grassroots organizations, and fostering environments where Indigenous voices are heard and respected.

Action also means education; it involves acknowledging how an intersecting series of social and political practices reserve visibility and power for some while marginalizing and silencing others.

This book also serves as a poignant reminder that justice is not solely the responsibility of Indigenous Peoples. It is a collective responsibility that requires the active participation of allies who are willing to stand in solidarity and amplify the voices of those affected. It calls for a dismantling of the structures that perpetuate violence and a sincere commitment to justice and healing.

This book is a call to action, a record of struggle, and a testament to the unrelenting strength of a people who refuse to be silenced. The poems, essays, and reflections within these pages invite us to see the unseen, to hear the unheard, and to remember the forgotten. Through words and art carefully sewn together by love, we are reminded of our inherent power to transcend boundaries, to heal, and to transform. The red dresses, like the collection of work on these pages, are both a memorial and a mandate.

In honouring the lives of those who have been lost, we also honour their families, communities, and nations whose strength and resilience inspire us to strive for a world where such tragedies no longer occur. This book is a testament to that strength, a celebration of that resilience, and a pledge to continue the fight for justice.

The power of grassroots activism, the strength of women, the resilience of Indigenous Peoples—these are the forces driving change in Canada. It is up to all of us to stand in solidarity with them, to amplify their voices, and to demand justice for the Missing and Murdered Indigenous Women, Girls, and Two-Spirit individuals whose lives have been lost.

The journey ahead is arduous, but it is one that we must make together, because we need each other.

Êkosâni kinanâskomitinâwâw.

IN MEMORIAM

Cathy

JAIME BLACK-MORSETTE

dip down into the heat
of your heart
the rhythm twice humming
in the ground beneath your feet

you place your hand
soft
on my shoulder
you held me in kindness
in gratitude
and i held you that way once
before you left
your body

Cathy

you left your body
because it was too small
to hold
the hurt
too small
to hold
your heart

as it grew and grew
big enough to hold us all

Gizhe-manidoo

Niin Keewatinoo Pinesi. Bizhiki nindoodem.
Gibi-nanaakomin noongom gaa-giizhigak.
Gakina nindinawemaaganag, nindaanikobijiganinaanig, owe bimaadiziwin gaa-bi-miizhiyaang, mii go gaye ingiweg awesiwag, giigoowag, ingiweg gaa-bimoodewaad gaye.
Owe gaye gaa-bagidinaamowaang, owe nibi wenji-bimaadiziyaang, owe aki wendanjigeyaang.

Noongom, nimbi-gaagiizondaan owe gichi-izhichigewin, REDress ezhinikaadeg. Gaa-onji-izhichigaadeg, ingiweg gaa-gii-wani'indwaa, gaa-gii-makamindwaa, ongoweg gaye gaa-medasawenimaawaad iniwen gaa-gii-wani'aawaad. Aya'aag gaye ongoweg begosendamowaad ji-gikendamowaad gaa-izhisenid iniwen, gemaa gaye ji-gwayakosijigaadenig.

Gizhe-manidoo, gigaagiizomin. Zhawenimishinaam ji-mashkawendamaang owe inake ji-bimi-izhichigeyaang.

Aho

Keewatinoo Pinesi

Creator (Great Spirit)

I am Northern Thunderbird of the Buffalo Clan.
I come to you today to give thanks.
For all my relations, our ancestors, for all the life that you have given that includes the animals, birds, fish, and insects.
Also for the air we breathe, the water that sustains us, the land that nourishes us.

We come today to ask blessings for the incredible project of the REDress. For all it stands for, those that have been lost, taken, those that suffer the loss. For those that continue in hope and prayers for closure and justice.

Creator, we humbly ask for blessings, strength, and resilience this day to continue this work.

Aho

Northern Thunderbird (Patti Beardy)

The power of our collective voice is a beacon for the rekindling of memory . . .

—JAIME BLACK-MORSETTE

Beginning

JAIME BLACK-MORSETTE

SINCE THE ARRIVAL of settlers on Turtle Island, Indigenous communities have been the target of violence, oppression, and genocide. Those that do not identify with or maintain colonial systems were and continue to be met with violence. Tellingly, those most affected have been Indigenous women, girls, and Two-Spirit people. We have always been on the frontlines in the fight to preserve culture, community, and connection in the face of colonial rule.

For thousands of years we have functioned in relative balance with each other and the natural world around us. Land-based cultures were able to sustain this balance by understanding and honouring our reciprocal, interdependent relationship with one another, the land, and waters. We still carry this understanding within us; we know what it feels like to act in right relation to each other, to create connection and show care, to take seriously our responsibility to support one another. Returning to the wisdom of our ancestors is a powerful antidote to colonialism—as we reconnect to land and water and reclaim spirituality, art, language, and space, we continue to unsettle the nation-state and grow ever stronger in who we are and what we are fighting for. The power of our collective voice is a beacon for the rekindling of memory, a reckoning with history, and a homecoming to a profound spirituality that holds sacred space for all life.

At the beginning of my path as an artist and activist, I was able to hear from renowned Two-Spirit community activist and sexual health educator Jessica Yee. What Jessica shared that day in Kamloops has stayed with me and informed my work for Missing and Murdered Indigenous Women, Girls, and Two-Spirit people (MMIWG2S) over many years. Jessica spoke of the reasons behind the high rates of violence against Indigenous women, girls, and Two-Spirit people. She reminded us that many Indigenous communities across Turtle Island before the onset of colonization were in fact Matriarchal, that women and Two-Spirit people have always been at the heart of our communities. We are the spark, the warmth, and the passion that draws together nations. There is an Anishinaabe teaching that fire represents the hearts of the women. It is this fire that has been under threat for over 150 years.

For myself and many others, the REDress Project has been a catalyst for reigniting this fire in our hearts. Through my work as an artist and advocate for MMIWG2S, I am honoured to be connected to a powerful community of women, girls, and Two-Spirit people, family members, artists, activists, scholars, and Knowledge Keepers, many of whom fill the pages of this collection with their voices and stories. These networks of women are our contemporary Matriarchy; we are an unstoppable force for change, reclaiming our position and power in a system that is built to silence us.

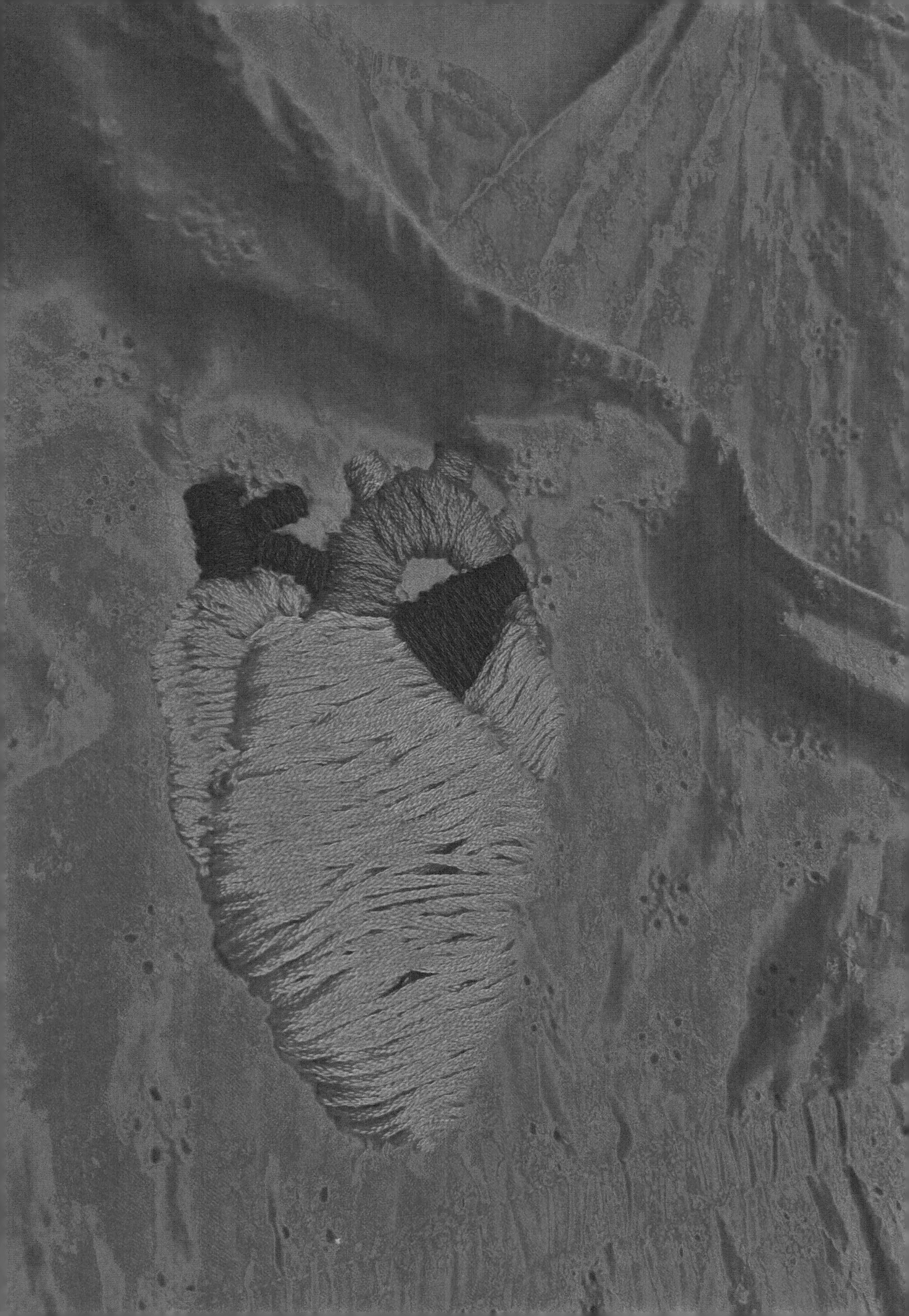

SHE LIGHTS A FIRE

My people will sleep for 100 years, but when they awake, it will be the artists who give them their spirit back. —LOUIS RIEL

Ishkode. Noodin. Aki. Nibi.
Ishkode. Noodin. Aki. Nibi.
Ishkode. Noodin. Aki. Nibi.

Ishkode. Ishkode. Ishkode. Ishkode.

THE BOOK OF JESSICA

At seventeen I am reading in the corner of the classroom, hair like a curtain of seclusion around my book; *The Book of Jessica*, by Maria Campbell. In it a young woman comes from the reserve to the city and faces a violent life of addiction and exploitation, the narrative lives on both sides of the veil, in the physical and the spiritual world… so close like they are almost one and the same. Jessica is nearly lost to herself, but it is her continued connection to the spirit world that holds her together, and it's this that I recognize, that I understand. I read the book over and over again. On the cover is a painting of an empty red dress.

Thumbing through the racks at a thrift store I find a red dress, an old floral print fabric, probably from the 70s. I buy the dress that day and keep it special until the spring. When I hear the thunders come I put on my red dress and walk barefoot out into the fields, the wind whipping my hair. I open my palms to the sky.

TALKING WITH THE THUNDERBIRDS[1]

Ya way ha-a ya-way ha . . . (6 drum beats)

Ya way ha-a ya-way ha
Ya way ha, ya-way ha
Ya way ha, ya way, ya-way ho . . . (6)

Binesi ginoona, binewaa ginoona
Binesi ginoona . . . Heya! . . . (6)

Ya way ha, ya-way ha, ya-way ha, ya-way ha
Ya way ha, ya way, ya-way ho

LIVING MEMORY IN THE PUBLIC SQUARE

The plaza in Bogotá, Colombia, is alive with people, a city square held in the embrace of lush green mountains. Zocalo, the centre. Here the women gather just as the sun begins to get high, first some, then more and more until there are one hundred, two hundred, nearly three hundred women standing together. They are here to call out the names of those they've lost, the disappeared, the murdered, those who spoke in defiance against systemic oppression, those who paid with their lives for speaking out.

The women—mothers, grandmothers, daughters, some as small as three or four—are all here together; their strength is in numbers, in connection, in community. They come together for all to see, they speak out for all to hear.

For hours the square is occupied, reclaimed by women dressed in purple, or shrouded in black, mourning the lost. A line of empty shoes tied together is slowly dragged across the square in honour of those who can no longer fill those shoes. A piano plays, filling the air; there are mournful cries, shouts of defiance, rage, grief, all coalescing into a crescendo. These women creating a tide, these women rising.

A drum sounds and a clutch of dancers dressed in red blooms at the centre of the circle, their bodies moving in perfect time with one another, telling a collective story of violence, grief, defiance; a murmuration of swirling red. And then the break, the discord, the dancers come apart, running in all directions, frantic, as though they are looking for their loved ones in that very moment, calling out their names.

A rush of red to the centre of the square and they are all helping one woman to climb to the top of the statue, standing looking out over the square in her red dress she shouts out:

Where Are They?

THE REDRESS PROJECT

In 2009, at an Indigenous Studies conference in Germany, the room is filled with German academics and a few delegates from Canada. Jo-Ann Episkenew, a professor from First Nations University of Canada in Saskatchewan, is there. I am on the sidelines, listening.

The Germans have a fascination with the Indigenous people of Canada, a fascination tinged with exoticization, a flattening of the real lived experience of being Indigenous in a country founded on colonial conquest.

After hours of presentation Jo-Ann stands up and speaks. She says, "There are over five hundred [the officially recorded number at the time] missing or murdered Indigenous women across Canada." The room is so silent, you could hear a pin drop.

It is when she says this that I imagine red dresses. Red dresses along city streets and in parks and trees, where every day the public passes by. Red dresses confronting people on their way to work, to school, to dinner. Red dresses as a stark reminder of all those we've lost. Red dresses to remember.

After listening to Jo-Ann speak and witnessing the women working together to call out violence in Bogotá, I knew that I must follow my calling. Being witness to the courage and integrity of the women fearlessly fighting for their communities brought me back to a part of myself that I had never accessed before. What had only been a flicker became a roaring flame: my voice, my creativity, and my spirit were ignited by the fire I witnessed in those women, and I became determined to carry that fire forward.

To REDress, to put right a wrong.

I am at the thrift store again, this time with purpose, looking for crimson, scarlet, burgundy, cherry; the reds that stand out among the other fabrics. I find seven dresses—cotton, satin, polyester, a gown; floor-length, a dress, long-sleeved and long at the hem, in a fabric light as air.

I gather these dresses and keep them close, care for them. It's winter and I bring them to the long boughs of a willow overlooking the river, place them in a group in the trees. The long-sleeved dress catches the wind first and like a dancer is animated. The other dresses sway in time. An old dance, the kind that you can only learn if you allow the wind to lead. And the dresses teach me this dance and I follow.

Over the next year more than one hundred red dresses are donated to me to begin this work. The donations come from far and wide, from Indigenous and

REDress; to
put right a wrong.

non-Indigenous people, from Europe, the US, and all across Canada, from Nunavut to the East Coast. As the dresses continue to come in I am invited to create large installations of red dresses on college and university campuses, at community organizations and schools all across the country.

Since 2010 I have created over one hundred large-scale installations of red dresses. The installations bring together community in circles that provide care, recognition, education, and ceremony. Circles that make space for the voices of those who work on the frontlines in communities to create a safer world for women, girls, and Two-Spirit people. It is an honour to be part of these circles and to see the ways in which women across the country are working to make change. It is an honour to carry this fire together.

TK'EMLUPS

I am on the VIA Rail to Kamloops, BC, with one hundred red dresses. Tk'emlups te Secwepemc territory, the Thompson River, turquoise and sprawling, flanked by high sand hills and gold grasses.

Thompson Rivers University (TRU) and the Tk'emlups band welcome me in, walk beside me, show me the spaces where we can have the dresses; in the young trees along the busy walkway, suspended in the entryway of the main university hall. We work together to make space for over seventy red dresses across the TRU campus.

Then we are driving to Tk'emlups band territory just outside of town. There, a community hall and the imposing brick and mortar of the Kamloops Indian Residential School. We park in the long shadow of the school and walk together around the corner into the bright of the setting sun. Elm trees line the front of the school; this is where we will put the dresses. I am ushered into the front doors. The people have reclaimed the building, made offices and cultural and community spaces there, but the halls are dark, and walking them I feel sick in the pit of my stomach.

Back outside we put the dresses in the trees, place them so they can catch the light and move with the wind. We put the dresses in the arms of these trees that have seen everything that has happened in this place... these trees that hold those memories.

Near the end of my time in Tk'emlups I am invited back for a community gathering honouring the REDress Project. There are men around the big drum and children in regalia zigzagging through the crowd. A grandmother Elder approaches me and takes both of my hands in hers. She looks me in the eyes, a look of great pride and gratitude, and says, "Don't stop doing what you're doing, my girl." We stand together as the drum begins and the people speak of all that has happened in their community—about the loved ones who have disappeared, the legacy of colonialism and violence and genocide that has led to so many missing or murdered women and girls. There are prayers and tears and songs and laughter and dance. I slip out the back to visit the dresses, to walk the line of trees where they dance together in the wind. On a tree right in front of the doors of the school there are three new dresses: a grandmother's, a mother's, and a child's red dress.

[1] Linda Beacham, *Maang Gonaandaagozid*, 4th ed. (2017).

Ontario Native Women's Association

Jaime Black-Morsette In Conversation with Judy Da Silva

BOOZHOO. DIBISHKOOGIIZHIGOOK NDIZHINIKAAZ. Bizhiw ndoodem. I'm Judy Da Silva from Grassy Narrows, and I'm Anishinaabekwe. Both my parents are Anishinaabe, and I'm from this area they call Treaty 3. Just thinking about your REDress project, it starts a lot of thoughts for me. One of them is the urgency of the women disappearing and being killed and being targeted. Being Anishinaabekwe with two daughters and a granddaughter, it makes me a fighter.

I'm Kookum and mom and auntie. And I'm auntie and Kookum to many, many women. And they are not all blood-related, so I feel that protection over them. Plus, I'm also a Lynx Clan, and historically the Lynx were protectors of the people. Before European contact, the Lynx were the ones that were the scouts of the people. So when the people were travelling all over the land, the Lynx Clan were the ones that went ahead first. They would go to see where the next good camping ground would be. Then, during wild rice season, they'd go find the good wild rice area. But during a time of war, they would say, "No, there's no enemy there, we can camp here."

Red is south, and when the birds go south, they come back with seeds in their mouth. When they fly back up north, they drop the seeds and new growth happens.

So that's the Lynx and that's the feeling we have. We served the blockade in Grassy Narrows in 2002, but things were already happening before 2002. When we were blockading the roads and stuff, when you looked at the people that are blockading, they're mostly Lynx people.

JAIME: Oh, interesting.

JUDY: And it wasn't even thought of. It just so happened that there were Lynx on the frontlines. I think that happens in a lot of Indigenous communities. That blood memory happens automatically. And that makes me think of you . . . that somewhere along your lineage there is that instigator or somebody that was in your bloodline.

It's really, really urgent what's happening with Native women right now. We, as Indigenous people, are at the frontlines of that devastation. To me, because of the residential school syndrome, our people kind of got brainwashed to be quiet and to accept things. It's like we've built a hard skin when devastating things happen. We're shocked and we're scared at first, like when they find a dead body or something. And then . . . and then our people have adapted so well that once the shock wears off, we move on with life.

JAIME: We keep going.

JUDY: Our people need to break that cycle and break "being quiet." We need to be more noisy and shake things up and not give up. It's like a cycle we keep going into with women dying. Our people are dying.

JAIME: Yeah, and people are scared to speak out, you know? Because it's so dangerous.

JUDY: This has a lot to do with the REDress project. Why it has to be in your face. Seeing how it's taken off all over the world, it's because the REDress Project has brought out the truth. And red, to me, means blood. But also red means protection, like in ceremonies. We say red is a protection. Red also means life. And what I've heard is red is south, and when the birds go south, they come back with seeds in their mouth. When they fly back up north, they drop the seeds and new growth happens. So it's like there are all of these meanings of red.

The REDress Project has taken off in so many, many different ways. I've seen with ONWA [Ontario Native Women's Association], they have a red jingle dress. You saw it right?

JAIME: Yes, I did see it.

JUDY: And the creator keeps it like a bundle. He has it in a suitcase and it has everything with it. It has a copper cup and it has tobacco in it. It has feathers. So his vision has built like a home, a sanctuary.

I feel like, when I'm talking about the racism, it's because of resources. We as Anishinaabekwe, we carry life. And because we carry life, we are nation-carriers. We carry the babies and then that baby will carry a baby. It's like a line of us that are coming and then that's why we're targeted. Because we are like a block for the resources that they want.

JAIME: Exactly. I feel like there's such a deep connection between violence against the land and violence against our people. It's the same thing.

JUDY: It's connected, yes.

JAIME: Just that feeling of entitlement and taking, and that aggression, right?

JUDY: Yeah, and then when you come to Grassy Narrows, you see how much empty land there is. There's so much water—like water you can swim in that's still clear.

JAIME: Yeah, it's amazing.

JUDY: And we're in the way.

JAIME: I know that things are bad. And what just happened in Winnipeg with those four women, after doing this work for so long, it just feels sort of disheartening that this continues on and on.

JUDY: When they found those four women, and when that guy was charged, the first thing that popped up was the little red dresses. People were cutting them and pasting them on their windows.

JAIME: Were they here?

JUDY: Yeah.

JAIME: It's like people are saying, "I'm an ally." That symbol has become a symbol of allyship. I think it also brings in people that are not experiencing this. It brings them into the conversation too.

JUDY: And the kids that are being raised like here, they see . . .

JAIME: And say, "Oh, what is that for?" And then suddenly there's a talk, and then there's teaching.

JUDY: Yeah. And maybe it opens up a different world to them that they wouldn't have had access to.

JAIME: I also think that people are starting to expect industries, organizations, and institutions to pay attention to what we have to say in a different way than they ever have before. Because I think there's more of a social pressure to listen. And to listen and to pay attention when we're speaking up about these things. And I feel like the dresses have done that too. They created a space. It's scary to speak out but it's less scary when you're doing it together, right?

JUDY: Absolutely.

JAIME: And it's safer to do it together. The more circles we make, the more we build that community, we can stand up together against these forces that are constantly trying to take our land and our people. It's hard to fight all the time. It's really hard.

JUDY: Yeah, and I think that's part of the REDress Project. It keeps it in your face kind of like, "Remember?" And the other thing now is Orange Shirt Day. You see the orange shirts hung up all over the place. So you can't forget.

JAIME: Yeah, you can't forget. Exactly.

JUDY: It's not just women, it's also young children and young boys too. My brother disappeared in 1985 in Winnipeg, and they never found him.

JAIME: How old was he?

JUDY: He was thirty to thirty-four, I think.

JAIME: Oh my god.

JUDY: Yeah, he disappeared and was never found. No trace, nothing. No indication of what happened to him. So we don't know, we have no clue. He still has an open case on him.

JAIME: Oh, my gosh.

JUDY: Yeah, so I have that understanding. I always put MMIWG**B** because I recognize that boys disappear too.

We as Anishinaabekwe, we carry life . . . we are nation-carriers.

JAIME: It's happening, yeah.

JUDY: In Thunder Bay I think there was like eighteen young boys that disappeared or showed up dead.

JAIME: Holy.

JUDY: So it's not just girls, it's also boys.

JAIME: What gives you hope in all of this? What keeps you fighting and what makes you feel connected?

JUDY: For myself, it's because I'm a survivor. I'm a fighter and I'm not a victim. That's in my heart, in my chest. So I try and pass that on to the other ones that are vulnerable. I try and give them that. What gives me strength, what gives me hope, is my fight in me and I try and give that to the young girls that are vulnerable.

JAIME: For me, I feel like the dresses are reclaiming space. They're taking up space at blockade sites where they're protecting the land. They're becoming warriors in that way and standing up like how we're trying to stand up too, you know?

JUDY: And it is in your face. Not in *our* face but in the culture's face.

JAIME: In the public eye, right? And I think that's just it. All this violence and colonialism, they just want everyone to forget about it and pretend it doesn't happen, because if it doesn't happen to you every day, you don't even know it's happening. And that's the first thing—being loud and saying, "This is happening."

THEY TRIED TO BURY US

There are things you
can only tell the wind,
low hum, wailing,
strong enough to
carry all the things
we couldn’t say.

— JAIME BLACK-MORSETTE

Ishkode. Noodin. Aki. Nibi.
Ishkode. Noodin. Aki. Nibi.
Ishkode. Noodin. Aki. Nibi.

Noodin. Noodin. Noodin. Noodin.

OPASKWAYAK CREE NATION

Before creating the REDress Project I spend a year in Toronto studying education. It is busy and competitive, packed streetcars and sidewalks where you have to walk with elbows out just to claim some space for yourself.

When the year is out I go as far away from Toronto as possible, to northern Manitoba. I accept a teaching position six hours north of Winnipeg, in Opaskwayak Cree Nation (OCN), The Pas. Up in the thick pine bush where the cold is colder and you can walk for hours without seeing anyone.

And I do, I walk the back skidoo and deer trails out by Big Eddy where the wind wails through the trees and the sky is a piercing blue. Past the old lodge all tied with coloured cloth tobacco ties and a glacial rock the size of a car, a sacred rock, a rock that, when you walk past it, feels something like a moment of vertigo, a warp in the air.

A lot of people I meet up here are named Flett, like the Fletts tied to my family line, and when we go out for a smoke they are quiet and observant like my grandpa always was, and the quiet is comfortable. But there is, too, a darkness in the silence, something so present but unnameable. A rift, a distrust, even a palpable fear, a divide even wider than the river that snakes between the town and the community of OCN on the other side.

There are two bridges over the river, one smooth concrete and steel and then the old train bridge right beside. People dare each other to cross it, and if you do you can see all the way down to the river through the gaps between the railway ties. Some even climb to the top of the black bolted steel girders—just to see things different, just for something to do.

One night, decades ago, a young woman and her friends crossed that bridge into town, and she never came back.

Her name was Helen Betty Osborne.

For over ten years no one came forward with any information against the men who killed Helen, even though it was known throughout town who they were. They kept on with their lives as though nothing had happened.

The women and girls from OCN tell stories of hiding when trucks passed as they walked home from school, knowing that it could be the men who murdered Helen. An entire generation of women, living in fear for their lives day after day. It is this that I feel everywhere I go.

At the grocery store and the gas station, along the roads, crossing over the bridge and especially out back in the bush, I can feel it. But still I go back there again and again, looking for something.

STRONG WOMAN SONG[1]

Way hay-a, way-hey-a hey-o

Way hay-a, way hay-a hay-o

Way hay-a hay hy o

Way hay-a ho way hay-a

Way hay-ya hay hy o

Way hay-a, way hay-a way hy o

Way hay-a ho way hay-a

Way hay-a way hy o

ONLY IN DARKNESS CAN WE SEE THE STARS

In 2014, the body of Tina Fontaine is found by the Alexander Docks along the banks of the Red River. Tina was just fifteen years old. A wave of grief and outrage shudders through the community, and there is a renewed outcry to take immediate action to protect Indigenous women, girls, and Two-Spirit people in our city. A community-led push to have a national inquiry into the systemic causes of violence against Missing and Murdered Indigenous Women, Girls, and Two-Spirit people (MMIWG2S) reaches a tipping point.

Red dresses are placed along with flowers and offerings by her family at the site where she was found. I visit this place, carrying red cloth ties or tobacco, a copper penny or a ring; others leave painted stones and medicines—beautiful things, sacred things for her.

I am asked to create an outdoor performance art piece on the banks of the Red River and I immediately know the story I need to tell.

I begin in the middle of the frozen river, wrapped in a white down quilt, a bright light over my heart illuminating the blanket from the inside out. White blanket on white snow, I am almost invisible. I slowly stand and walk along the river, appearing only as a faint light in the distance. As I walk closer to the bank, the glow of the light grows stronger and my presence becomes tangible.

SEARCH THE LANDFILL

Morgan Harris
Marcedes Myran
Rebecca Contois
Mashkode Bizhiki'ikwe

In the spring of 2023, the city of Winnipeg is shaken by the news that four Indigenous women were murdered and that their remains are believed to be located at a landfill site just south of the city. Family is notified, and the process to lay charges against the man responsible begins.

As though the grief and the shock are not enough, the police and the Province of Manitoba refuse to search for the remains of the slain women. The families of the victims and their community supporters are forced from shock into action.

A call for justice is led by the daughter of one of the slain women—Cambria Harris, daughter of Morgan Harris. A camp is made in a large open grassland near the landfill site; it is called Camp Morgan, named after Cambria's mother.

At first the camp is a lone tipi in the snow where a sacred fire is lit, never to be extinguished until the remains of the women are found. The fire is tended day after day, by one and sometimes two fire keepers, through the blistering cold winds that shriek across the fields on the outskirts of town, as all the while the dump trucks continue day by day to carry and dump the city's trash at the site.

Supporters work together to gather and display over one hundred red dresses at camp and around the landfill site. For four square miles along the fence line, red dresses stand together blowing in the winds.

Members of an Edmonton community support organization arrive at Camp Morgan with 155 more red dresses to donate and display at the site; one dress for every year since the confederation of Canada.

Cambria Harris is in meetings and negotiations with the city and province; she is invited but not listened to, welcomed and ignored at the same time. The possibility of support is extended over and over again but no action is taken.

I go to the police headquarters and hang a single red dress in front of the building.

Rallies and community events are organized. We gather at the intersection of Portage Avenue and Main Street, at the very heart of Turtle Island, all dressed in

red. We are three hundred strong, our drums echoing the heartbeat of the land, our voices rising together.

Someone breaks from the group and begins painting red right onto the street. Others join in, filling the entire intersection with red. Slowly the shape of a dress is formed, a one-hundred-foot-tall red dress.

[1] Linda Beacham, *Maang Gonaandaagozid*, 4th ed. (2017).

BANK OF MONTREAL
SEARCH THE

Red dress woman, will be found.

Red Dress Woman

CAMBRIA HARRIS

Red dress on the fence
Fire in the ground
Wondering where you went
If you're safe and sound

Medicines in my hand
Wind talking in the air
On this sacred land
I'm sending you my prayers

Creator will bring you in
For you are not alone
Oh our red dress women
We will bring you home

Your spirit lives on
Your presence shakes the ground
You live on through nature
You are safe and sound

Red dress woman, will be found.

SEARCH THE
LANDFILL

WE ARE HUMAN
NOT
TRASH

Bring Me Home

CAMBRIA HARRIS

The landfill is our home
While we lay alone
Waiting for them to find us
In the garbage dump

Someone put me here
For some reasons
I don't know why
But for now I lay within
Until the government decides

To find her and I
Why must this be the fight
My own family
Cannot sleep at night

My daughter cannot reach me
Until they tell her yes
For she will be arrested
If she tries to put me to rest

I fight for my mom
Until she has a voice
Until they finally find her
Until we can rejoice

No landfill is a grave
It's been done before
Why is it different for indigenous
Why do you close the door

Your thinking is all excuses
For all the reasons not to; why . . .
To delay our human rights?
Until you can decide?

Strip us of more won't you?
You've stolen it all.
Taking our women, watching us fall.

I wait for my daughter
Like I always have
While we couldn't in the living
This is your chance

I am not a story
I was and am loved

Remember that as the wind blows
As you hear the voice above
Above and within
The wind of all life
This is and will be my fight

Bring me home
#searchthelandfill

Vanish

GLADYS RADEK

A portion of this piece was previously published in *Reclaiming Power and Place: The Final Report of the National Inquiry into Missing and Murdered Indigenous Women and Girls.*[1]

THROUGH A MOTHER'S WOMB another baby girl was born. Our beloved Tamara Lynn Chipman—TLC—and her spunky character won the hearts of our large extended family. She soon became the apple of Grampa's eyes as she grew faster than the hair on her head. If nobody knew where she was, we always knew she was with Grampa at their usual table at the West End Restaurant where all the old boys would be hanging out and teasing her because of her bald little head and huge smile with twinkling eyes. Grampa would fiercely defend her when they called her a boy! Her hair eventually turned into curly little locks of brown at the age of four. She grew up holding Grampa's stories in her heart. He passed away when she was still very young, but she never forgot.

TLC loved her daddy too; she stole his heart from the moment she was born. Even her mom knew she would always be a daddy's girl forever. With the loss of her Grampa, she clung to her daddy, became his little shadow. She loved the fishing boats, fast cars, and dogs and led an adventurous outdoor life in northern Canada. She was never afraid of anything, lived life to the fullest, and she grew into a tall, lanky, charming, beautiful young lady with a smile that would brighten anybody's day. She blossomed from being daddy's little tomboy to a young mother at age nineteen.

They say there is no pain greater than a mother giving birth. The greatest pain is the fear of losing that child after giving birth, should the truth be told. TLC's greatest fear was realized when she had her little boy. She feared ever losing him;

they bonded forever and more. Her father, once again, had the twinkle in his eye as he enveloped his heart around his little grandson, a spitting image of his once little TLC and yet another wonderful addition to our already large extended families. This child, too, was loved, cherished, and valued by all of us. We shared stories about how the antics of our babies reflected on us when we were young. We laughed at the way our children are an extension of us and bring us so much joy.

Then, out of the blue, something out of the ordinary happened. There were no phone calls, no knocks on the door, no cheery hellos. No more "Hey Daddy, what are we going to do today?" All of a sudden our world came crashing down. Nobody had heard from TLC. A few days went by and it slowly turned into weeks, a month, and then into years.

Her disappearance created so much pain in our family as we resorted to search parties through the mountains, along the railroad tracks, in ditches and culverts, and treaded through the back alleys of communities where angels wouldn't dare tread. We have searched local, provincial, national, and international waters for our baby girl, only to realize that there were so many more. The heartbreaking reality is that Canada has a dark little secret. That little secret is the overwhelming numbers of Missing and Murdered Women and Children in this country that nobody wants to acknowledge.

When TLC disappeared it was time to take some serious actions to raise awareness about her and the thousands of Missing and Murdered Women across this country. The heartbreaking reality is that Indigenous women and girls are twelve times more likely to be murdered or missing than any other women in Canada.[2] National walks and awareness-raising campaigns were brought to life by a group of grassroots activists in Vancouver, BC. These grassroots activists are the frontline workers who have dedicated their lives to the most vulnerable people in society. Those who have fallen victim to all forms of violence: sexual assaults, childhood trauma, residential schools, exploitation, prostitution, and drug and alcohol addictions. These frontline workers have been mopping up the blood of our women 365 days a year, 24 hours a day, 7 days a week. No forms of violence take days off.

First call of action was to demand a national public inquiry. Our gracious prime minister honoured our walkers by sending out a House of Parliament representative, who in turn told us he would ensure appropriate steps would be taken to follow our documented demands. Absolutely no follow-up from the Office of the Prime Minister since then.

TLC is our first thought every morning as we wonder where she is. The pain of not knowing leaves a huge hole in our hearts. The eternal flame will continue to burn in the hopes that someday soon she will bound in that door and say, "Hey Daddy, what are we going to do today?" Instead we wonder: is she warm, is she safe, is she alive, is she being held against her will, is she being raped or tortured, is she being bought or sold? What happened to her? Is she dead? Somewhere out there someone knows something. Prayers someday they will come forward and tell us the truth. This thought runs through the minds of all the families of our missing loved ones. There are thousands of us who wake up to this nightmare every single day.

So many people out there are using our loved ones' names and pictures for their own benefits. Organizations claiming they are there for the families, yet failing to contact the family who is in mourning. Lawyers lining their pockets through the judicial process that is protecting the rights of serial killers here in Canada over the rights of the women and thousands of children who have fallen prey to this dysfunctional and corrupt system.

The Government of Canada as a whole has the responsibility of ensuring each and every citizen is protected by law by implementing the United Nations' Universal Declaration of Human Rights for everyone. We should be protected by law through the ministry of public safety, from the top levels of government to the attorney general and solicitor generals provincially. The serious flaws with the police and the judicial system, and the lack of concern for even one missing or murdered woman, creates a distrust with the families. Few resources are made available to the families when their searches continue for years and decades. No resources are available for that family to heal from their broken hearts.

Most hurtful is the racism displayed when our Indigenous loved ones disappear. People say things like, "Oh, is she Indigenous?" "I heard she was just a party animal," "Was she wanted by the cops?" or the worst of all, "She lived a high-risk lifestyle." The latter could mean anything from prostitution, to addiction to drugs, to hitchhiking. None of which pertained to TLC or many of the other young girls and mothers who have simply disappeared. This stigma is perpetuated by the media that labels all our Indigenous girls and women this way, convincing mainstream society that all our women and girls are just that—prostitutes, addicts, and hitchhikers—and thus not worthy of searching for. For other ethnic groups the media portrays them in a totally different light: that they were excelling in school, popular, loved, valued, and missed.

Racism also dominated the widely publicized trial of Robert Pickton, leading us to the public inquiry and recommendations in *Forsaken: The Report of the Missing Women Commission of Inquiry*. Corruption and cover-up riddled the process right from the beginning. Today, the forty-nine-plus victims, their families, and the seventy-eight children whose lives were directly affected by this severed system will never get the justice they so richly deserve. Yes, it is admitted that many officers dropped the ball, and that stigmatization of high-risk lifestyles and racism played a significant role in the decisions, but this system failed to address proper accountability from any of those officers. Many files remain sealed so as not to implicate the many high-profile witnesses who either knew, or participated in, what happened at the notorious "Piggy's Palace."

Many don't realize that the women and girls did not stop going missing or being murdered after the arrest of Robert Pickton. Canada's prison system boasts serial killers that we, the taxpayers, are housing at this time. Each of them get three square meals a day, a roof over their heads, hydro, heat, clean laundry, full-benefit health care, education, counselling, phones, computers, drugs, protective custody, and security 24/7. All of these things our women and children struggle for every day.

What will it take to turn this system around? All of our women and girls should be treated with the same respect as the prime minister's mother, wife, daughter, or niece. What would he do if one of his family members were to simply vanish?

[1] National Inquiry into Missing and Murdered Indigenous Women and Girls, *Reclaiming Power and Place: The Final Report of The National Inquiry into Missing and Murdered Indigenous Women and Girls* vol. 1a (2019): 17, https://www.mmiwg-ffada.ca/wp-content/uploads/2019/06/Final_Report_Vol_1a-1.pdf

[2] NIMMIWG, *Reclaiming Power and Place*, 7.

Who

GLADYS RADEK

Who is that forlorn little child?
Reaching out in despair?
Love me, hold me, hug me
Almost like you care
Tisn't so bad
When there is feeling in the air

Her heart is sad and lonely
Craving for that love
The Great Spirit had created
From somewhere up above

Who is that child?
Crying in the night?
Violated of her womanhood
She is only taught to fight
The burden she is carrying
Invisible to the light.

Who is this child?
Crying in pain.
Willing someone to love her
To make her who again.

Who is this child crying in the night?
Who?

A Love Letter to My Grandmother, Mary Alice Martin

LEE-ANN MARTIN

Dear Totah,

I have long wanted to contact you even though you passed away seven years before I was born. This letter is my attempt to express my feelings for you and to share memories of my mother and our family since you've been gone.

I know you only through the few stories that Mom, your daughter Ola, told us about you as I was growing up. Mom spoke with great love for you, coupled with immense sadness that she was taken away by the Children's Aid Society and placed in the Belleville Orphanage at an early age, losing connection with you and her siblings. Yellow roses always proved to be a very haunting memory for her as she recalled your gardening prowess at home in St. Ola when she was a little girl. She repeatedly told us about the last time she saw you while at the orphanage. Apparently, she was feeling ill and so was placed in the infirmary where she looked out the window to see you walking away from the building. Mom understood that you had come to see her, but were turned away because she was sick.

It's painful for me to think about how you passed and how I never got to truly know you. To realize that you were living on the streets and found murdered in Trenton in 1941 when you were only forty-eight, and that we never found the person who did this to you. It's tragic to comprehend the pain and anguish that you experienced in trying to live your life after the loss of your younger children who had been taken by the Children's Aid Society.

Totah, you will be so happy to know that despite what she had to endure, Mom's strength and determination ultimately provided her a long and happy life. Fortunately for her, as a ward of the Children's Aid Society, she went to live with the Cronk family on what became her beloved Bay of Quinte. Jeannette and Frank Cronk grew to love her as a daughter, and Mom became close with their only son, Roy, who she regarded as her brother. Following graduation from high school, she moved to Toronto and later joined the Canadian Women's Army Corps during World War II.

In 1945, she married a man named Cliff Partridge, who was the brother of Mom's friend in the Army Corps. She and Dad raised three of your grandchildren—myself, my sister Suzanne, and my brother Scott. Mom was always very enthusiastically involved in our activities and sports. One of my fondest memories is of Mom sitting in the cold seats of the arena, knitting me skating outfits while I practised on the ice.

Surprisingly and wonderfully, Mom was able to keep in touch with many of your other children, especially her four sisters, Mae, Sadie, Bea, and Joyce. We enjoyed many family reunions, weddings, and other gatherings throughout the years since they reunited. Uncle Lloyd connected with them later in my lifetime, so he enjoyed family get-togethers for a short time as well.

I very much regret not having more conversations with Mom about you and her early life with her brothers and sisters. It's only been in the last few years since Mom's death in 2016 that I have come to realize how much I missed talking to her about you.

Too late I send you my love and respect. I pray that you found some peace in your passing.

Much love from your granddaughter,
Lee-Ann

"I Feel Like My Spirit Knows Violence"

Understanding Genocide—and How to Stop It—in the Context of the National Inquiry into Missing and Murdered Indigenous Women and Girls

KARINE R. DUHAMEL

INTRODUCTION

In June of 2019, the historic National Inquiry into Murdered and Missing Indigenous Women and Girls released its Final Report. The product of decades of advocacy by family members and survivors, as well as a Call to Action from the 2015 Truth and Reconciliation Commission of Canada, the National Inquiry was, in its construction, mandate, and output, an unprecedented undertaking. Comprised of fourteen concurrent inquiries—one in each province and territory, alongside one federal inquiry—those who worked within it had less than three years to investigate the broadest mandate ever provided to an inquiry in Canada.

I worked as director of research for the National Inquiry, from April of 2018 until the conclusion of its mandate in June 2019. Working with a research team across the country, we drafted the Final Report, as well as directed the work of the Legacy Archive and managed the Forensic Document Review Project. With a background in human rights research, I knew that our challenge would be to go beyond the statistics and lofty ideas and to ground our work in real lived expertise, offered through testimony, artwork, and dialogue, that told the real story of violence facing Indigenous women, girls, and Two-Spirit and transgender people in Canada. The Final Report focused on these accounts, providing an important human lens through which to examine the issue in a new light.

Within the context of that work, I saw first-hand how bravely confronting the truth as shared by those with relevant experience could change the lens through which we, as a society, see violence. Collectively, then, these voices engage a different collective memory—one that is not about a gradual weakening or disintegration of Indigenous bodies, families, and communities, but rather one that fundamentally rallies to understand violence in new ways, as an active process of dispossession, dehumanization, racism, sexism, and of genocide. The strength in the stories of survivors and family members also points to the way forward through Indigenous resilience, power, and place. What can they tell us about the nature of violence against Indigenous women, girls, and Two-Spirit and transgender people in Canada, and how does it reframe the pathway toward understanding violence, and its related solutions?

PART 1: A FINDING OF GENOCIDE

The National Inquiry's mandate was to investigate and report on the systemic causes of all forms of violence against Indigenous women and girls, including sexual violence, as well as to examine the underlying social, economic, cultural, institutional, and historical causes that contribute to the ongoing violence against Indigenous women and girls in Canada. The mandate also directed the National Inquiry to investigate and report on existing institutional policies and practices to address violence, including those that are effective at reducing violence and increasing safety.[1] There was no start and end date to our investigation and no specific lens through which to define violence, apart from the expertise of those who participated in the Truth-Gathering Process.

The National Inquiry was based on the idea that those with the most insight and expertise were, in fact, those who had lived experience—family members and survivors of Missing and Murdered Indigenous Women, Girls, and Two-Spirit and Transgender people. As such, part one of our Truth-Gathering Process focused on the lived experiences of those who came forward as family members and as survivors themselves. Witnesses had several options to share their truths, including within the context of Community Hearings, by providing a statement, or through submission to the National Inquiry's Legacy Archive. The archive collected artistic expressions, either through donations (from family members of missing and murdered loved ones, intergenerational survivors, and those working toward reconciliation), education projects, or acquisitions from artists and storytellers with an interest in the subject.[2]

Parts two and three of the Truth-Gathering Process grew out of the topics and issues that families and survivors identified as important to them. Part two hearings featured institutional expert witnesses and inquired into the systemic causes of institutionalized violence, as well as institutional responses to violence. Part three involved expert and Knowledge Keeper hearings and featured other experts—Elders, academics, legal experts, frontline workers, young people, specialists, and others—who provided their recommendations on systemic causes of violence and possible solutions.[3]

Prior to the release of the National Inquiry's Final Report, key media outlets were already buzzing about the National Inquiry's finding of genocide. On May 31, 2019, major media outlets including the CBC and APTN reported that a leaked advance copy of the Final Report included a finding of genocide. The genocide finding, from the Final Report, reads as follows:

> The violence the National Inquiry heard about amounts to a race-based genocide of Indigenous Peoples, including First Nations, Inuit and Métis, which especially targets women, girls, and 2SLGBTQQIA people. This genocide has been empowered by colonial structures, evidenced notably by the Indian Act, the Sixties Scoop, residential schools and breaches of human and Indigenous rights, leading directly to the current increased rates of violence, death, and suicide in Indigenous populations.[4]

As we heard from survivors, family members, and other experts, genocide encompasses a variety of both lethal and non-lethal acts, including acts of "slow death."[5] These acts have very specific impacts on Indigenous women, girls, and Two-Spirit and transgender people. While the National Inquiry acknowledged that the definition of formal liability was to be made by judicial bodies, its report, based on thousands of accounts, was well-positioned to lay the groundwork.

Genocide is defined in the United Nations' Genocide Convention as

> any of the following acts committed with intent to destroy, in whole or in part, a national, ethnical, racial or religious group, as such: (a) Killing members of the group; (b) Causing serious bodily or mental harm to members of the group; (c) Deliberately inflicting on the group conditions of life calculated to bring about its physical destruction in whole or in part; (d) Imposing measures intended to prevent births within the group; (e) Forcibly transferring children of the group to another group.[6]

Further, in Canada, the Crimes Against Humanity and War Crimes Act defines genocide with one further element, omission or the failure to act, as constitutive of genocide.[7]

Unlike the traditional paradigms of genocide, such as the Holocaust (twelve years), the Armenian Genocide (eight years), and the Rwandan Genocide (three months), settler colonial genocide takes place over centuries. For the National Inquiry, then, genocide in Canada can be understood as a composite act that includes several elements over a long span of time that, collectively, have the same impact. It is possible to conclude that, because of the overall pattern of state-funded or state-conducted violence, the ultimate goal of the policy or policies of the state cannot be anything but destruction, in whole or in part, of the targeted group.

In the wake of the release of the report, several prominent voices chimed in to undermine this finding. For instance, then Conservative leader Andrew Scheer argued that the level of violence directed at Indigenous women and girls in Canada should not be labelled a genocide, noting that "the ramifications of the term genocide are very profound. That word and term carries a lot of meaning. I think the tragedy involved with missing and murdered Indigenous women and girls is its own thing, its own tragedy, and doesn't fall into that category of genocide."[8] Others chimed in too, suggesting that the Commissioners and report drafters had not understood the term or its history and were leveraging its import for impact.

The narratives that underpinned the denial of the genocide finding were not surprising to those of us who are Indigenous, or who have worked in proximity to the structures of colonization that continue to generate violence to this day. How outsiders have "known" Indigenous people is a complex collection of supposition, stereotype, and myth.

As part of the underpinning structure, Indigenous women and girls have long been imagined, understood, and defined through a colonial gaze. In the Final Report, we draw attention to a process that is referred to as gendered colonization. While colonization "refers to the processes by which Indigenous Peoples were dispossessed of their lands and resources, subjected to external control, and targeted for assimilation and, in some cases, extermination,"[9] gendered colonization draws attention to the way in which these events specifically target Indigenous women, girls, and Two-Spirit and transgender people. Further, we emphasize the idea that colonization is a structure that includes "many different events—all created under the same, destructive logic."[10] Moving beyond colonization as a series of events to viewing it as a complex structure whose foundational elements are relatively stable means understanding how gendered colonization has jeopardized the safety of Indigenous women, girls, and Two-Spirit and transgender people in distinctive ways and in policies, practices, and stereotypes that were put into place long ago.

As the Final Report makes clear, the structures of colonialism must be identified to be challenged. From those that relate to the supervision and containment of Indigenous people, such as relocation, over-policing, or ghettoization, to those that operate to dehumanize people and to reduce Indigenous women, girls, and Two-Spirit and transgender people to stereotypes that are easy to dismiss, structures matter. The policies and practices that operate within them—such as the undermining of cultural knowledge and practices, the reduction of lands that sustain Indigenous knowledges or a distinctive way of life, and physical violence—all threaten the very survival of Indigenous communities and fuel distrust between settler society and institutions and Indigenous Peoples. Witnesses before the National Inquiry frequently cited systems-level change, as well as change at the individual and societal level, as important to address the legacy of colonization and to dismantle it in the present. A key example of this includes policies applied to First Nations such as the Indian Act, which tied a woman's Indian Status—and therefore her access to reserve land and resources—to her husband, and which has worked to disenfranchise Indigenous women and their descendants since its first iteration in 1876. It still exists today. Other examples, such as forced sterilization, criminally high rates of child apprehension, and over-policing and over-criminalization of Indigenous people, families, and communities, represent the actions informed by a superstructure that insists that Indigenous people are fated for extinction and that works to perpetuate this prophecy.

PART 3: CHANGING THE NARRATIVE: OUR WOMEN, GIRLS, AND 2SLGBTQQIA+ PEOPLE ARE SACRED

For those who appeared before the National Inquiry, generating dialogue about new spaces for creating safety must be founded not on the dehumanization of Indigenous women, girls, and Two-Spirit and transgender people, but on a celebration of their value, based in our assertion that "Our Women and Girls are Sacred." As Audrey Siegl, a member of the National Inquiry's health support team and supporter for the Elders and Grandmothers Circle, explained, "For our young women, for our grandmothers, for our women who travel with us, we are sacred because we exist. We are sacred because we have survived."[11]

As an illustration, rather than focusing on how a loved one was targeted for violence, families and survivors of Missing and Murdered Indigenous Women, Girls, and Two-Spirit and Transgender people who testified before the National Inquiry began by speaking about what made their loved one special, sacred, and so very much missed. For instance, Gwenda talked about her daughter, Amber, who dreamed of being a police officer or a teacher and who has been missing since the age of nineteen. Amber had been a pipe holder—a great honour in First Nations communities—and loved to dance powwow. Gwenda recalled watching Amber dance while wearing regalia designed and made for her by her father: "It was so amazing to see her glide as she lifted up her shawl. It was like she was flying like an eagle, soaring like an eagle when she danced, and her footwork, as she danced, every step was so light."[12] Becky M., daughter of Deidre, explained that her mother "had a great sense of humour and her smile would brighten a room. I know she had great love for those around her... I've always said my mother is more than what happened to her."[13] A loved one appeared on behalf of their relative, Jennifer C., and explained how on the day Jennifer disappeared, she had left a note for her mother, Bernice, that demonstrated her loving character. It began with "My beautiful mother" and ended with "I love you so, so much. X's and O's."[14] These women were sacred—they mattered. As Anthony explained of his sister, Michelle, "She was my second mother. She was the one who gave me haircuts, the one who made me dinner when I was hungry, the one who I looked up to, the one who made my birthday special, the one who loved and looked after me when no one else was around to."[15]

In addition to these personal accounts, and to further explore the concept of the sacred nature of Indigenous women, girls, and Two-Spirit and transgender people, the research team also undertook a study of traditional stories. For instance, one of the most widely known Indigenous Creation stories is that of Sky Woman, or Awe(n)ha'i' ("mature blossoms"). This is the Haudenosaunee (Iroquois) story of the pregnant woman who fell from the sky and who is helped by the many animals already living here to survive.[16] In the story, the great Turtle provides her with a place to land, and "after she turns a tiny bit of mud into vast land all along the Turtle's back, Sky Woman takes seeds from her hair and dances, sings, and drums the first plants and medicines into creation. She does this as an act of reciprocity, to show thanks to the animals who treated her with kindness and respect."[17] Beyond this, though, Sky Woman also leads a creative process that results in the existence of a place where the people can live; Sky Woman's work generates an unbreakable connection between the people and the land. Sky Woman's daughter, She Who Always Leads, then gifts the Haudenosaunee with their three staple foods: corn, beans, and squash.[18]

In the Haida story "The One They Hand Along," a young woman is kidnapped by the killer whale chief and taken to his home at the bottom of the ocean. Family members go to rescue her, including two female supernatural beings partnered with her brothers. These are Mouse Woman and a woman who is likely the mythical Xaalajaat, or Copper Woman.[19] Ultimately, it is Copper Woman who turns the tide at the critical moment. While the rest of the family cowers and loses faith when they confront the headman's family under the sea, Copper Woman stands up and insists that the family find their power. Copper Woman's biggest gift to the family, in this story, "was not a weapon, an item, or even secret knowledge. The gift she gave them was to remind them of the power they had all along. Like the inevitable return of the tide, their courage returned as well, and they were able to successfully negotiate their daughter's return."[20]

As illustrated in testimony and in storywork, then, culture represents the truest expression of what safety can and should look like. As Audrey Siegl shared: "Our connections to our ways, our teachings, our medicines... we see time and time again... those connections save lives."[21]

To support these connections, in early 2019 the National Inquiry's educational team created an art action project in collaboration with artist Jaime Black-Morsette that engaged territory- and Nation-specific teachings such as these. The ReClaim project combined "the aspect of remembering murdered or missing loved ones with the concept of 'calling forth,' implying a more active, ongoing engagement with not only the memory of those lost, but with the sacred teachings and connectedness that can ultimately help contribute to safety and to healing."[22] This project aimed to reassert presence and power on the land itself as a way of reclaiming the sacred feminine and asserting how our women, girls, and Two-Spirit and transgender people are sacred. It also created opportunities for families, women, and youth to come together to reconnect to the Matrilineal knowledge across different Indigenous communities.[23] In acknowledging the ways in which colonial genocide has sought to tear Indigenous people from their cultures and communities with significant and distinctive impacts on Indigenous women, girls, and Two-Spirit and transgender people, the ReClaim project, along with many other community-based healing projects presented before the National Inquiry, remains the most unexplored aspect of the work we did, and a necessary foundation for what must come next.

CONCLUSION: WALKING FORWARD, AND WHAT WE'VE MISSED

Since the end of the Inquiry, I've been dismayed by the delays and by the limited lens within which governments have interpreted the Calls for Justice and the path forward. Both the truth of genocide as well as the sacred value of Indigenous women, girls, and Two-Spirit and transgender people demand more and should prompt some big thinking beyond ontological and epistemological frameworks that themselves sustain violence.

As family members and survivors showed us, the foundation for safety must be stopping the dehumanization of Indigenous women, girls, and Two-Spirit and transgender people. This means confronting ongoing stereotypes, prejudices, and discrimination that place those most targeted as undeserving of safety and peace. In addition, understanding the issue of violence as an ongoing, rather than historical, violation of the rights of Indigenous people is key. As rights-bearers as well as those who hold responsibilities, women, girls, and Two-Spirit and transgender people, as well as all Indigenous people who live in Canada, must be supported by programs, policies, and legislation that honour these rights in international, domestic, and customary contexts. Finally, centring policy and programmatic solutions for violence within the context of healing and cultural grounding can provide a roadmap for what happens next. As the Final Report documented, there are so many programs designed and run by Indigenous communities and organizations that can make, and are making, a difference. Supporting these programs on a long-term basis, with predictable, stable funding and the reduction of bureaucratic red tape, is of primary importance. So, too, is the responsibility of each and every non-Indigenous person in Canada to find their role in supporting the reclamation of power and place for Indigenous people as true allies, transforming encounters that may harm to those that can heal for long-lasting and sustainable change.

The roadmap provided by the experts with lived experience can and should fundamentally alter how we see solutions. Rather than solutions being state-designed and state-driven, the implication is rather that solutions must be generated in community, adapted to particular realities and distinctive needs, and delivered by Indigenous people. Understanding how Indigenous women, girls, and Two-Spirit and transgender people are sacred, and understanding the importance of these roles and responsibilities, generates a strength-based and sustainable approach to addressing violence and ending genocide.

[1] National Inquiry into Missing and Murdered Indigenous Women and Girls, "Our Mandate, Our Vision, Our Mission," accessed August 15, 2024, https://www.mmiwg-ffada.ca/mandate/.

[2] National Inquiry into Missing and Murdered Indigenous Women and Girls, "Legacy Archive," accessed August 15, 2024, https://www.mmiwg-ffada.ca/commemoration-art-and-education/legacy-archive/.

[3] National Inquiry into Missing and Murdered Indigenous Women and Girls, *Reclaiming Power and Place: The Final Report of The National Inquiry into Missing and Murdered Indigenous Women and Girls* vol. 1a (2019): 62, https://www.mmiwg-ffada.ca/wp-content/uploads/2019/06/Final_Report_Vol_1a-1.pdf.

[4] NIMMIWG, *Reclaiming Power and Place*, 50.

[5] Justine Berezintsev, Katherine James, Laurel Rush, and Gabrielle Vallières, "Missing and Murdered Indigenous Women and Girls in Canada: Gender, Indigeneity, and Genocide," *Hypotheses Forccast* (2020), https://forccast.hypotheses.org/files/2020/10/Final-Paper-MMIWG-and-Genocide.pdf.

[6] United Nations General Assembly, Convention on the Prevention and Punishment of the Crime of Genocide, January 12, 1951, 78 UNTS 280, https://treaties.un.org/doc/Publication/UNTS/Volume%2078/volume-78-I-1021-English.pdf.

[7] Crimes Against Humanity and War Crimes Act, SC 2000, c 24, https://canlii.ca/t/543mm.

[8] John Paul Tasker, "It Is 'Its Own Thing': Andrew Scheer Disagrees with Indigenous Inquiry's Genocide Finding," *CBC News*, June 10, 2019, https://www.cbc.ca/news/politics/scheer-mmiwg-genocide-1.5169000.

[9] National Inquiry into Missing and Murdered Indigenous Women and Girls, *Reclaiming Power and Place: Executive Summary of the Final Report* (2019): 231, https://www.mmiwg-ffada.ca/wp-content/uploads/2019/06/Executive_Summary.pdf.

[10] NIMMIWG, *Reclaiming Power and Place: Executive Summary*, 233.

[11] NIMMIWG, *Reclaiming Power and Place*, 41.

[12] NIMMIWG, *Reclaiming Power and Place*, 79.

[13] NIMMIWG, *Reclaiming Power and Place*, 105.

[14] NIMMIWG, *Reclaiming Power and Place*, 649.

[15] NIMMIWG, *Reclaiming Power and Place*, 109.

[16] NIMMIWG, *Reclaiming Power and Place*, 150.

[17] Ibid.

[18] See Kim Anderson, *A Recognition of Being: Reconstructing Native Womanhood* (Toronto: Second Press, 2000).

[19] NIMMIWG, *Reclaiming Power and Place*, 160–61.

[20] NIMMIWG, *Reclaiming Power and Place*, 161.

[21] NIMMIWG, *Reclaiming Power and Place*, 147.

[22] NIMMIWG, *Reclaiming Power and Place: Executive Summary*, 47.

[23] Ibid.

Calls for Justice for All Canadians

An excerpt of the Calls for Justice from *Reclaiming Power and Place: The Final Report of the National Inquiry into Missing and Murdered Indigenous Women and Girls.*[1]

As THIS REPORT has shown, and within every encounter, each person has a role to play in order to combat violence against Indigenous women, girls, and 2SLGBTQQIA people. Beyond those Calls aimed at governments or at specific industries or service providers, we encourage every Canadian to consider how they can give life to these Calls for Justice.

We call on all Canadians to:

15.1 Denounce and speak out against violence against Indigenous women, girls, and 2SLGBTQQIA people.

15.2 Decolonize by learning the true history of Canada and Indigenous history in your local area. Learn about and celebrate Indigenous Peoples' history, cultures, pride, and diversity, acknowledging the land you live on and its importance to local Indigenous communities, both historically and today.

15.3 Develop knowledge and read the Final Report. Listen to the truths shared, and acknowledge the burden of these human and Indigenous rights violations, and how they impact Indigenous women, girls, and 2SLGBTQQIA people today.

15.4 Using what you have learned and some of the resources suggested, become a strong ally. Being a strong ally involves more than just tolerance; it means actively working to break down barriers and to support others in every relationship and encounter in which you participate.

15.5 Confront and speak out against racism, sexism, ignorance, homophobia, and transphobia, and teach or encourage others to do the same, wherever it occurs: in your home, in your workplace, or in social settings.

15.6 Protect, support, and promote the safety of women, girls, and 2SLGBTQQIA people by acknowledging and respecting the value of every person and every community, as well as the right of Indigenous women, girls, and 2SLGBTQQIA people to generate their own, self-determined solutions.

15.7 Create time and space for relationships based on respect as human beings, supporting and embracing differences with kindness, love, and respect. Learn about Indigenous principles of relationship specific to those Nations or communities in your local area and work, and put them into practice in all of your relationships with Indigenous Peoples.

15.8 Help hold all governments accountable to act on the Calls for Justice, and to implement them according to the important principles we set out.

[1] National Inquiry into Missing and Murdered Indigenous Women and Girls, "Calls for Justice for All Canadians," in *Reclaiming Power and Place: The Final Report of the National Inquiry into Missing and Murdered Indigenous Women and Girls* vol. 1b (2019), 199.

how does change come

JAIME BLACK-MORSETTE

how does change come
like lightning
urging the earth to fruition

boughs shifting
under the weight of plenty

a new root sent out
into the histories of the earth

hands touch
grit under fingernails

I sometimes remember and sometimes forget
how a breath is a current
a currency
carried on a cold front
to the frontlines

where the rage of a century of injustice
splits the silence

tectonic plates shifting to make space
for the voices that go unheard

the rise and fall
dizzying
the hands clutched tight
to the rattle
to the drum

or

is it slower
like the timing of a resting heart
our collective pulse
open vein of the land
a river
that will never run dry

SHE HOLDS GROUND

When you feel like you are falling, know that the land can hold you steady, remind you of what you are made of.

—JAIME BLACK-MORSETTE

Ishkode. Noodin. Aki. Nibi.
Ishkode. Noodin. Aki. Nibi.
Ishkode. Noodin. Aki. Nibi.

Aki. Aki. Aki. Aki.

THE LAND CARRIES US

They say that when it's all too much to carry you can lean on the land. The land, of course, is strong enough to carry us all. When you feel like you are falling, know that the land can hold you steady, remind you of what you are made of. I know this, or at least I've heard this, but I am on the road, headed east down Highway 17. Gitchigami; Lake Superior, Lake Huron.

I am running from something, running to get out from under something that is crushing me, running to finally catch my breath. I am running like my mother ran, like her cousins and aunties had to run. Running is in our blood; it's why we're still here. When I arrive at camp I am welcomed in; they are harvesting wigwas. The river runs too, laughing. I lie belly down on the ground and curl into an indent on the land and for two, three, four days, I let the land hold me. Let it keep me from falling.

My aunty tells me we are first from the Anishinaabe around the Great Lakes area in the time of Chief Peguis. She tells me that some from our family line followed him from here to the Red River Valley, that same migration from the Great Lakes to the heart of Turtle Island, where the rivers meet at the forks—a path I have travelled over and over my whole life.

When I travel this path, I remember who I am. I return to these lands again and again because they remember me as much as I remember them.

RED RIVER

footfalls to where the rivers split
or merge
where the sun sets, rises
where everything turns red
where the footfalls of the ones who went before
echo or fit
my footprint

here where the muddy water
conceals our shadows and catches the light
cloth ties taken by wind
moving colour, woodsmoke
our hands on the clay
tell stories the land remembers
tell stories without speaking
the wind becomes our words
coming in gales
shake tent, eagle wing, salt tears

We dream the revolution
We dream the revolution

HOME/BODY, HOME/LAND

This river clay holds our history, the slow water reflecting the light that lives in us. Walking the banks feels like walking in the footsteps of the ones who came before, and if you look close you can even find traces, fragments of that history.

Remnants of the vessels made by the hands of our ancestors, red clay marked by their fingertips from ten thousand years ago. To touch these fingerprints with your own feels like a homecoming, a reconnection to land and body, a taking back of what's been stolen over and over again.

THUNDERBIRD HOUSE

I am invited to a ceremony at Thunderbird House in Winnipeg, a clay ceremony. Led by Christi Belcourt and Isaac Murdoch. In ceremony we are marked with clay, fingertip to forehead, and this meeting of body and land feels like a marriage, a reconnection to a beloved; this relationship to the land made physical through the act of painting onto the body.

In this moment I feel a deeper connection, a renewed responsibility to stand for the land and waters, to make a commitment to care for and protect and in return be cared for and protected.

I think of the connections between our human bodies and the land itself, how our veins are small rivers that rush and wind through us, keeping us alive . . . just as the rivers rush through the fields and valleys of the land. How the branches of our lungs are like the branches of the trees, filtering the air so that we can breathe, and the quiet lakes and pools of clear waters like our wombs, able to support and sustain life. How our bodies and the land have both been sites of violence and conquest, how reclaiming this body, my body, this land, my land is my quiet way of saying, “No more.”

No Land Was Seized

ZOEY ROY

I don't want to go back there anymore
It wasn't me to begin with
I was let down, burdened, bound, and unheard
So what I looked for something calming
To make sense of the hurt
I don't want to hate myself no more
I know now that disdain is something I learned
A social prison
Like addiction
Not something I earned
But traits burned into my mind
To tell me who I really am
A faceless dime piece
Programmed for the man
How convenient
They were wrong
We were taught that way
Told girls like me
Were a blind spot
In the back way
Dwelling in the shadows
In need of a fix
How compelling

For the shallow ones
To concede amongst kids
I won't smile for them anymore
Fawn for self protection
Negated by self-neglect
I demand my own respect
Command myself
To reflect on the truth of the matter
Dissect the players and their game
So I can stop the chatter
Get a hold of my laughter
Of my peace
Of my love
Show myself there is an after
And I will always rise above
Cuz I'm here
Writing this
And I'm in one piece
Mostly sober n' healthy
And, now I'm in reach
Things are happening for me
That gives me a sense of ease
Even with my disease to please
I've maintained my own vitality
I often need a hug
Even with my fear of touch
I'd do anything for love
As long as I could be enough
I speak from experience
So my sisters in it deep
Can know there's a life for them
Beyond the chaos of the streets
It's their voice that says you're weak
We as women from this land
Are more than they could perceive

That's why it's up to us
To be firm in our belief
Of who we know ourselves to be
look at all that we can do
Us, together, in our truth
We are the living proof
Pain and all
We are the land beyond perception
We are planted here
On purpose
A sacred conception
From our roots
We are guided
This body was for me

The Power of Red and The Power of Community

CHRISTI BELCOURT

IN THE SUMMER OF 2022, Maria Campbell, my dad Tony Belcourt, and I were travelling together, and we had the opportunity to visit some relatives in the Métis communities of Lac Ste. Anne and Edmonton, Alberta. Although I had never lived in Lac Ste. Anne, my dad was born in the community, as were my grandparents and many generations going back. Many decades ago, Maria had visited Lac Ste. Anne. As we were chatting back in the hotel room, she told me about a film she had made in 1978 called *The Red Dress*.[1] It was filmed in Lac Ste. Anne. I became excited to see it because Métis people from there were apparently in the film as extras. She wondered aloud if the National Film Board of Canada still had the film available for viewing online, so I logged onto their website and lo and behold, it was.

I sat enthralled as we watched it. And there, in one of the scenes as the camera panned across the inside of a local bar in Alberta Beach, which is the little village down the road from the Métis community, I saw a dozen or more Métis people from our community. It was a typical 1970s bar and one that I hear hasn't changed all that much since then. While we were watching the film, for a very brief moment I caught a glimpse of my chapan (great-grandmother) Madeleine Letendre (née L'Hirondelle). She was sipping on a beer, and also appeared in that same scene a bit later dancing with her husband, John Letendre. And even though the film dealt with sexual assault, displacement from our lands, and the impacts of colonialism on our cultural identity and how that foreshadowed our awareness of what has become a crisis of murdered and missing Indigenous people, seeing my chapan come to life on film, even briefly, was healing for me.

How my chapan Madeleine survived into old age is a mystery to me. Her husband, John, was violent, mean, a heavy drinker, and the kind of man everyone knew "girls are not safe" around. My nohkom (grandmother) Matilda L'Hirondelle was my chapan's first-born, and she was not John's biological daughter. My nohkom was raised by her grandparents as it wasn't safe for her to be in the home with John. My grandmother's sisters, his biological daughters, were also sent to be with their grandparents from time to time for that same reason. I never got to meet my chapan in person because my mom and dad and us kids were living in Ottawa, but when I sat down in that hotel room with Maria and saw her in the film, through Maria I got to "meet" her in a new way. I got to find out that it was her and the other "old ladies" at Lac Ste. Anne who Maria spent time with who encouraged her to make the film and to tell the story of what happened to our people. They spent a lot of time together, and I now treasure the memories Maria has shared of her.

In the story of *The Red Dress*, the main character, Kelly, is a "Métis man without treaty or hunting rights, struggling to sustain his traditional life."[2] His daughter, Theresa, is a budding artist whose dream is to go to France to study art. She dreams of a red dress, which is symbolic of her dreams because her grandmother raised her to believe if you dream for something, you always put out red cloth as an offering. So, according to Maria, "the dress becomes the symbol of her desire to become an artist, to represent her people. Her lands are being clearcut and she believes it's her way of being able to help. She believes that if she has that red dress she will be a good artist and will be able to help her dad speak for her people and her lands. She longs for it as she believes it will somehow be the power she needs to make her dream come true."[3]

In the film, we see Kelly, Theresa's father, sell his beaded jacket that his mother made for him. The jacket also being symbolic of traditions, knowledge, and power. His mother made it for him as medicine. She put her prayers into the stitches. She believed it would help to make him stronger when he met with government officials. A government agent sees the jacket, like they see our lands, and convinces Kelly to sell it. With the money he gets from the jacket, he purchases the red dress for his daughter, thinking she simply wants it to go to a graduation dance. He didn't understand she viewed the dress as her medicine power, as older generations often don't understand younger ones. Kelly forces his daughter to go to the dance, mad that he sold the jacket for this dress that she doesn't want to wear to the dance. Theresa is sexually assaulted, and there is more to the story, but within the overarching theme of the film, the red dress is a symbol of both medicine power and loss.

I asked Maria why she decided to title the film *The Red Dress*. She answered, "The red dress was a symbol that if we became spiritually grounded, we would be stronger to make change. I always had a red dress hanging in my closet all my life. I would never wear it. My auntie had a red dress—she never wore it either. Why did you decide to use a red cloth under the vamps in Walking With Our Sisters? Why did Jaime decide to hang up red dresses? It means all of us are working toward a spiritual meaning. That red cloth helped us all to find a way. It's like blood memory. One thing we have in common is the colour red. Our blood creates; our menstrual cycle—we are two-leggeds, we are humans, nothing else. That's why it's so powerful. That is the food that feeds our babies for nine months. In Cree the word for red and blood is the same: mihko. It's the only colour that carries that kind of word to describe it. mihkoyan—I'm bleeding. Blood is where life begins. Blood is where it forms. Red is the colour of creativity. It's Creation itself—the most powerful thing of all when your body creates a human."

From that first film *The Red Dress* to the Red Power movement, to Jaime Black-Morsette's REDress Project, to Walking With Our Sisters, to the red hand placed across people's faces, and more recently people in the Search The Landfill actions in Winnipeg on September 18, 2023, who were all wearing red T-shirts—red is the colour of the movement. Red has become the de facto colour of the MMIWG2S movement and other actions for justice for Indigenous people.

Red has long been viewed as a colour of power and strength, and red ochre as a pigment continues to be used in our ceremonies to this day. The earliest known harvesting site of red ochre in North America dates to nearly thirteen thousand years ago.[4] Prepared in recipes that included fats of different kinds of fish or animals, red ochre paint has endured thousands of years in rock paintings and as a preservative used in burials. Today many people continue to use red ochre as a pigment painted on sacred ceremonial items or on faces, and we use the colour red in a variety of spiritual practices and ceremonies in the form of red cloth. More than any other colour, red has found its way into an expression of power, grief, strength, and solidarity in this movement, a movement mostly led by women, for

"The red dress was a symbol that if we became spiritually grounded, we would be stronger to make change."

—MARIA CAMPBELL

an end to violence against Indigenous people on a whole. We make a spiritual connection triggered by the colour red, which is the colour of birthing, menstruation, creativity, life, and death, with midwives helping both processes of bringing life into this world and helping people be birthed into the afterlife. We have used red ochre on the bodies in preparation for burial, in ceremonies; something is being stirred in us so we don't give up hope.

Using red cloth on the ground underneath the moccasin tops in Walking With Our Sisters (WWOS) was a natural choice. WWOS was a commemorative installation, which the public was invited to attend, of over two thousand pairs of moccasin tops (sometimes called "vamps") placed in rows on top of red cloth that covered the floors of the museums, art galleries, universities, and community halls. We had only one goal of the project: to honour the lives of those missing or murdered. All involved agreed to be guided under four main principles for the project: 1) To do the work under the leadership of Indigenous grandmothers and Indigenous ceremony; 2) That everyone is treated with kindness and gentleness, no matter what the circumstances are; everyone is welcome and everyone is equal; 3) The space is nonpartisan and nonpolitical; everyone is a human being first—all affiliations and statuses are left at the door; and 4) Everyone is a volunteer, no one is paid, and no profits can be made from any part of the project.

WWOS travelled to twenty-seven different communities between 2013 and 2019 when we held the final ceremony. It was estimated that over sixty thousand people had attended the events over the seven years. Thousands of people had served as volunteers in each community, and at each location the event was a ceremony guided by their Elders, following the traditional protocols of those regions. We transformed institutional spaces into temporary sacred spaces, insisting that it was Indigenous women who would lead it from start to finish following regional ceremonial protocols. We challenged the norms of how things are done in galleries and institutions by centring prayers for MMIWG2S and their lives and insisting that no one would be acknowledged for the elected positions they held; there would be no opening speeches—only Elders conducting ceremony. In some spaces, institutions had to adjust or rewrite their rules so that Indigenous spiritual ceremony could be accommodated and be conducted at the time of day, for the length of time, and in the ways needed—such as not asking the Elders to curtail the ways in which they needed to follow their own protocols in ceremony, like the use of smoke in pipe ceremonies or smudging. We asked them to let us lead and essentially take over and use their spaces as we needed, and to their credit, the leadership of those spaces generously did everything they could to adapt to what we needed, even if it caused trepidation and nervousness on their part at first. The cause was the common goal, and people were aware of the issue Canada-wide. In some communities, the relationships built between the institutions and the local Indigenous communities were strengthened long after WWOS left their territories.

Over the seven years that WWOS travelled, many pipe ceremonies were held, many songs were sung, much tobacco was offered, and tens of thousands of people walked on the red cloth path as they viewed the vamps. I believe the red cloth helped to ground people and give them strength as they bore witness to the enormity of the horror of murdered and missing Indigenous women in North America. So many prayers were made for an end to the violence in our communities, for the families and loved ones of those murdered to be comforted in their grief, and for those still missing to be found safe and to come back home.

Visitors who entered WWOS were invited to smudge upon entering the space, carry tobacco in their hands to offer in prayer for the families of those murdered or still missing, and walk along the red path—on top of the cloth, shoes removed, heads bowed to the floor and walking softly and carefully with each step as they looked down at pair after pair of moccasin tops, meticulously placed, row after row forming the colour of a rainbow. The enormity of the expression of love that you could feel coming through the energy of what was created, combined with the enormity of the loss we face in our families, communities, and nations, moved many to tears. The energy emitted from the art created was palpable. I believe in each thing we do we transfer energy to what we make, and in so doing, we can affect others. Having good thoughts while beading, cooking, or making something is important as a sign of respect and love for others who might come into contact with what you've made.

At the time when I made the first call-out for people to send me vamps in 2012, the Native Women's Association of Canada (NWAC) had been documenting the cases of murdered and missing Indigenous women for several years, collecting stories and interviewing family members, and creating a national database.[5] By March of 2010 NWAC had documented 582 known cases of Indigenous women or girls who had been murdered or who remained missing.

Based on this information, my goal was to collect roughly 600 pairs of moccasin tops for the Walking With Our Sisters installation. In 2012, I asked several people to help me form a National Collective[6] to manage the project and made a WWOS public group page and a public post on Facebook inviting anyone to send me pairs of moccasin tops. By the time the first installation opened in Edmonton in September 2013, we had received an unexpected and staggering 1,763 pairs. And during the years WWOS was travelling, that number expanded to well over 2,200 pairs, including 600 pairs of children's vamps sent in by family members to represent the lives of Indigenous children who did not make it home from residential schools. The response was overwhelming and heartfelt.

The first ceremony with the children's vamps was held in Sault Ste. Marie at the site of the old Shingwauk Residential School (now Algoma University). The Children of Shingwauk Alumni Association, those who had survived residential school, had the idea to make a call-out for children's vamps to commemorate the children who never returned home from those institutions. The children's vamps became the centre focus, placed together with the Eagle staffs, for every installation following that one.

We used social media as a tool to crowdsource everything we needed to organize the project, including our funding. We did not accept any government funding or resource extraction money for any of the installations or the tour. We fundraised on social media with Facebook "auctions" and donated 50 percent of everything we raised in our auctions to other groups who had been doing the work with MMIWG2S families and youth for years, such as Tears4Justice, Two-Spirited People of Manitoba, Families of Sisters in Spirit, the Native Youth Sexual Health Network, Maisy's Foundation of Hope, Butterflies in Spirit, Awasis Sacred Journey, and Got Bannock. We wanted to do things differently from the norm and try to support other groups leading the movement and making huge strides at the grassroots.

WWOS began and ended as a project of compassion and demonstrated the power of community. The project changed and morphed over time, from what we thought was an art installation into exercises of community strength, determination, compassion, and action, and expressions of Indigenous grandmothers' leadership. This became especially important as an act of rematriation[7] in places where patriarchy has particular strongholds.

In the long history of the movement for an end to violence for Indigenous women and families, there isn't one catalyzing moment we can all point to and say, "Ah, yes, that is when the revolution started." All generations are seed planters for the next.

Those who find themselves on the frontlines of grassroots movements for justice and change come from all sectors and vocations. Sometimes as artists we use our art in service to the cause. In the same way, Indigenous people who are lawyers, teachers, professors, designers, writers, advocates, models, and so on also use the tools they've been given in service for the people. We are all in this together, and we all wear multiple hats to try to achieve change.

Seeing the vamps for the first time all laid out on the red cloth, the night before the opening, I walked the path for the first time and became overwhelmed with the emotions of understanding the issue of MMIWG2S started centuries ago. The statistics we use today are only based on the last thirty years. How many women? How many children? How many men? How many Two-Spirit and nonbinary people? How many of our people for the last four hundred years? We are not only the survivors of genocide, but as Pamela Palmater states, the genocide against Indigenous people by Canada continues:

> So why is it so important to understand the history of genocide in Canada? Because it's not history. Today's racist government laws, policies and actions have proven to be just as deadly for Indigenous peoples as the genocidal acts of the past. What used to be the theft of children into residential schools is now the theft of children into provincial foster care. What used to be scalping bounties are now Starlight tours (deaths in police custody).[8]

When I was asked to write this article on WWOS to demonstrate the connection between art and activism, I struggled to write it because I don't really know how to articulate the connection between the two. That seems too abstract for me to wrap my head around. I do know that WWOS wasn't "art as witness." Nor was it created to "raise awareness." It provided a vehicle for a collective expression of compassion and grief for community, by community, and with community. Anyone who came and had their awareness raised as a result was a side-bonus. For me it was always about providing space for our own people, our own communities.

The moccasin tops were intentionally not sewn into moccasins, to represent the unfinished lives of those taken from our communities and families before their time. Much of the artwork on the vamps spoke to the issue of loss and grief by highlighting the absence, the vacancy left by the violent removal of a loved one in people's lives.

WWOS was from its beginning more than art, but looking at the artistic aspect of the project specifically I would describe it as "art within action for change"—it's art that existed within an existing movement for change, it didn't create anything. The people had already done that. But WWOS provided an additional way for people to express their grief and compassion through the art they created. It's similar to Jaime Black-Morsette's REDress Project in this regard, where now hanging a red dress is a way to express solidarity with the movement and express a collective call for action.

Similarly, Maria Campbell's film *The Red Dress* in 1978 wasn't separate from the other work she was doing on the ground with other sisters—creating safe houses, participating in decades of action on issues that ranged from ending violence to family advocacy, to protecting land, to mentoring young people and artists to pick up the mantle. She always worked in collectives and never worked alone.

As Indigenous people we don't stand outside this issue as observers. We are fully in it, feeling the effects in our families and communities. Violence against Indigenous people has affected each and every Indigenous person. We have used and will use every tool available to us to end the violence including art, film, literature, oral tradition, and taking back language. And red will always be the colour of power.

Maria told me that my great-grandmother, my chapan, encouraged her when she was there in Lac Ste. Anne doing the film. She said my chapan was at her house just about every day, and all the "old ladies," including her and her sister "Old Lady Letendre," were behind her all the way. Maria spent time with her, having tea and driving her around. Because I never got to meet her, this precious memory is one I will take with me. And it reminds me that we never do this work alone. Each generation must mentor and encourage the next to pick up where we left off.

Power to the people.
And as Maria says, "Power to the babies!"

[1] Maria Campbell, *The Red Dress* (National Film Board of Canada, 1978), https://www.nfb.ca/film/red_dress/.

[2] Campbell, *The Red Dress.*

[3] Maria Campbell, all quotes from personal conversation with the author.

[4] Kamila Kudelska, "A study confirms the oldest red ocher mine in North and South America is in Southeastern Wyoming," *Wyoming Public Media*, May 27, 2022, https://www.wyomingpublicmedia.org/open-spaces/2022-05-27/a-study-confirms-the-oldest-red-ocher-mine-in-north-and-south-america-is-in-southeastern-wyoming.

[5] Native Women's Association of Canada, "Fact Sheet: Missing and Murdered Aboriginal Women and Girls," accessed June 18, 2024, https://www.nwac.ca/assets-knowledge-centre/Fact_Sheet_Missing_and_Murdered_Aboriginal_Women_and_Girls.pdf.

[6] The National Collective for Walking With Our Sisters was formed in 2012. Maria Campbell was our lead Elder and advisor. Other members of the collective included myself, Natalie Bertin, Lisa Shepherd, Tanya Kappo, Tara Kappo, Erin Konsmo, Lisa Periard, Dr. Savage Bear, Tracie Louttit, Kara Louttit, Rebecca Beauline-Stubbing, Theresa Corky Larsen Jonasson, Lynn Jonasson, Doreen Roman, Christine King, Tracey Pawis, Connie Greyeyes-Dick. With periodic advisors Tony Belcourt, Shane Belcourt, Gregory Scofield, Sherry Farrell Racette, Maria Hupfield, and Ryan Rice.

[7] Rematriation is a broad term being used by this author to describe the re-centring process of recovery and restoration by Indigenous women of Indigenous women's practices, Matriarchal governances, knowledges, and land-based practices on behalf of themselves, their families, and communities.

[8] National Inquiry into Missing and Murdered Indigenous Women and Girls, *Reclaiming Power and Place: The Final Report of The National Inquiry into Missing and Murdered Indigenous Women and Girls* vol. 1a (2019): 53, https://www.mmiwg-ffada.ca/wp-content/uploads/2019/06/Final_Report_Vol_1a-1.pdf.

Nikâwiy Nitânis

MACKENZIE ANDERSON LINKLATER

STORYTELLING HAS ALWAYS been my main source of research and inspiration when it comes to my work as a visual artist. I've been very fortunate throughout my life to have relationships with my mother, grandmothers, aunties, and cousins, that are grounded in care and laughter. Visiting with my loved ones is an act of knowledge transmission that has allowed me to learn my familial history. This history and the kinship between women is the focus of my practice.

My grandmothers on both sides of my family are Nihithow Iskwewak from northern Manitoba. My paternal grandmother, Charlotte Anderson, is from Misipawistik Cree Nation with ties to Pinaymootang First Nation. My maternal grandmother, Rose Linklater, is from O-Pipon-Na-Piwin Cree Nation. My mother was raised up north with Cree being her first language. She would tell my brother and me stories of summers spent at fish camp, the anecdotes of life on the trapline, and the visiting that was central to that way of being.

When making *Nikâwiy Nitânis*, I reflected on the relationship of motherhood and caregiving. This painting interprets the Matrilineal connection between a mother and child at the spiritual level. The spirit lines flow throughout, intertwining the two figures and connecting them to each other and all of creation around them. Our first mother is the earth, and I felt called to acknowledge the life she and other parents give. Teachings I've received are grounded in the understanding that all of creation holds spirit, and all our relations should be treated

as such. With this understanding I created *Nikâwiy Nitânis* in response to the violence toward Indigenous women, girls, and our Two-Spirit relatives. I wanted to emphasize our spiritual connection and how deeply it is felt when our relatives are taken from us.

Heart Work

JAIMIE ISAAC

A BEAT OF THE DRUM emulates the mother's heartbeat, a deep resonance of life affirming. The heartbeat, voice, and experiences are heard and felt by the child yet to be born. Elder Margaret LaVallee said that language is learned in utero and mothers are the first teachers. As life givers, mothers and women have a significant gift and role to play in community, roles that should be upheld and cherished, yet women and children face disproportionate violence and poverty in today's society—an enduring gift from colonialism. Colonialists rejected Indigenous worldviews and disrupted respectful relationships and relational ways of living on this land. Poignantly simplified, "Indigenous women and Two Spirit people were the first targeted by colonial and religiously rooted violence, which was wielded to access resources and lands," and emphasizing further,

> highlighting the matriarch structure of many Indigenous nations, Seneca organizer Iako'tsi:rareh Amanda Lickers... also explained the lasting effects of the violence that Indigenous women frequently experience: "women carry our clans and... by carrying our clans, [they] are the ones that hold that land for the next generation... so if you destroy the women, you destroy the nations, and then you get access to the land."[1]

Colonialism created the Indian Act, policies that legislated disenfranchisement, stealing our children and land that led to culture and language loss, sexism, and gender-based inequality felt and fought today. This was/is the antithesis of a matriarch-based, traditional, pre-colonial governance that honoured and held women in high esteem. The Indian Act legally controlled what Indigenous Peoples could do and determined the status of Indigenous women in every part of their lives through the oppressive legislation, setting in place the destructive relationships between Indigenous women in Canada and the Crown and injuring the heart of families by disrupting traditional motherhood practices. In 1951, Canada's Indian Act was amended so that the compulsory enfranchisement and the ban on important cultural ceremonies like the Potlatch and Sundance were dropped, and in 1960, Indigenous people secured the right to vote.[2] However, inequality for gender-based policy continued.

My mother, both an intergenerational and residential school survivor, had to give up her Treaty Status after marrying my father in 1977. She fought for her rights to obtain her status back with support of Bill C-31 in 1985, which eliminated discriminatory provisions. Indigenous women who married non-status men no longer lost their status. But during the years of treaty loss, she lost any supports and her rights to land in her community were severed. The laws for Indigenous women have been continuously stacked against them, which has created conditions of patriarchal control, societal disadvantages, disrespect, and rampant hate crimes against women and children. My mother, Elaine Isaac (née Courchene), and grandmother Mary Courchene, who are both residential school survivors, are two of my Matriarchal sheroes, diligently advocating for the rights of Indigenous children in the child welfare and education systems. As a social worker and therapist, my mom knew some of the women and children later missing or murdered, which she was heartbroken about, often taking home the weight of her work through her stress. When identifying cracks in the systems and questioning the colonially built structural issues, she broke the rules and courageously resisted to make better decisions for the children in care. She shared stories of her days working with women in domestic abuse situations where a man pulled a gun on her and she stood her ground, often having to work with the police to mediate. Despite her childhood trauma and stressful career, she had the heart of a lion, fierce with a sense of justice and care.

My nana, a teacher, school administrator, and Anishinaabe language advocate, worked to make significant differences and positive change in the education system and was the first principal of the Children of the Earth School, a self-determined urban high school for Indigenous students. Early on in life, I saw these women caring for children in social work and schools as a way of righting the wrongs that were inflicted on them from the residential schools; as a way of healing through their careers and community with unsurmountable stress. My mother took me to community-organized protests and walks since I was a baby. My nana, her sister Aunty Bebs (Margaret LaVallee), and their friends organized a community walk to the legislature in 2011—A Grandmother's Walk to Protect our Children in downtown Winnipeg. I was asked to photo-document the walk. Witnessing intergenerational strength and resiliency through Indigenous Matriarchal voices and visions of a future that protects children was impactful and affirming. Indigenous people mobilizing their political will and empowering their communities through awareness and advocacy is powerful.

The colonial-based child welfare and justice system started with the residential school policy, the Sixties Scoop, and continues now as a broken system that routinely fails to protect children and youth in care and in incarceration. A systemic cycle of trauma and institutional control is a colonial system meant to contain and suffocate, disrupting traditional and cultural connections to family and homelands. Child advocates and federal government statistical reports show that more than half the children in Canada's foster care system are Indigenous,[3] so separation of families is still a colonial agenda as the causes are related to intergenerational trauma and legacies of colonial policies; poverty, addictions, violence, and state denial of these atrocities leads to a general devaluation of and racism against Indigenous people. The devaluation of Indigenous lives is expressed in silencing, dismissal, violence, and aggression—micro and macro in everyday situations.

In 2014, Tina Fontaine was a fifteen-year-old girl from Sagkeeng First Nation whose body was found in the Red River, a tragedy no one should ever forget. Her death sparked an outcry of emotion and injustice. Fontaine was in the child welfare system, her short life of endured intergenerational trauma cut short without justice. In the aftermath, Tina Fontaine's death left a legacy of action; a National Inquiry into Missing and Murdered Indigenous Women and Girls (NIMMIWG) would commence. Community-based initiatives for justice and protection like Drag the Red, led by the forcible MLA Bernadette Smith and Bear Clan Patrol/ Mama Bear Clan Patrol, brought people together with grassroots efforts. In 2023, Cambria Harris with a group of supporters launched the Search The Landfill campaign/plea for the government to support the search for her mother, Morgan Harris, as well as advocating for Rebecca Contois, Marcedes Myran, and Buffalo Woman (a respectful attribution to an unnamed woman), who are believed to be in Winnipeg landfills. Cambria Harris filed a complaint of discrimination under the human rights code against the Progressive Conservative Party that denied the request. Cambria is a young adult and mother who is passionately and courageously fighting for the dignity and respect of her mother and all those who are missing and murdered. Her fight has won the ears and hearts of so many, including Manitoba's first Indigenous premier, Wab Kinew. Indigenous-determined political and social agency has raised consciousness and broadened mainstream awareness to the point of critical mass and action—change is achievable. The Indigenous-led governmental bodies the Assembly of Manitoba Chiefs and the Southern Chiefs Organization continue to exercise their political support for First Nations communities and have grassroots connections and self-determined advocacy for their community.

Art also has a transformative power to affect, to change, and to move people irrevocably. As a mixed heritage/Indigenous Anishinaabekwe curator, I reflect on impactful artworks and exhibitions that have deeply resonated with me, established powerful positionalities that subverted colonial knowledge, confronted white privilege and Western-centrism, challenged and resisted heterocentrism and sexism, and flipped the patriarchal gaze. One particular work that shook me to the core, left me thunderstruck and quite literally in tears, is Rebecca Belmore's magnificently organized exhibition Facing the Monumental, curated by Wanda Nanabush. I witnessed *The Named and Unnamed*, a video projection of Belmore's 2002 performance *Vigil*, held on streets in Downtown Eastside Vancouver that were known sites of abduction. In a red dress, Belmore labours to tear off and hammer the dress to a hydro pole while heart-wrenchingly screaming women's names that are written in black marker all over her arms. After each name she holds a thorned rose through clenched teeth. At the end of the performance, in jeans and T-shirt, Belmore leans on the omnipresent black pickup truck playing (oddly one of my favourite songs) James Brown's "It's a Man's Man's Man's World" from its stereo. Two of the many names she screamed happened to be the names of my sister and mother, and hearing them in that context presented a terrifying comprehension of loss.

Another experience with artwork close to home was with an exhibition I co-curated called Insurgence / Resurgence at the Winnipeg Art Gallery in 2017. We commissioned Casey Koyczan for a site-specific work, where for days he onerously collected driftwood from the riverbanks of the Red and Assiniboine Rivers in Winnipeg and carefully assembled them as a hanging structure—a mobile of interconnected branches bound together with twine and wire to represent missing

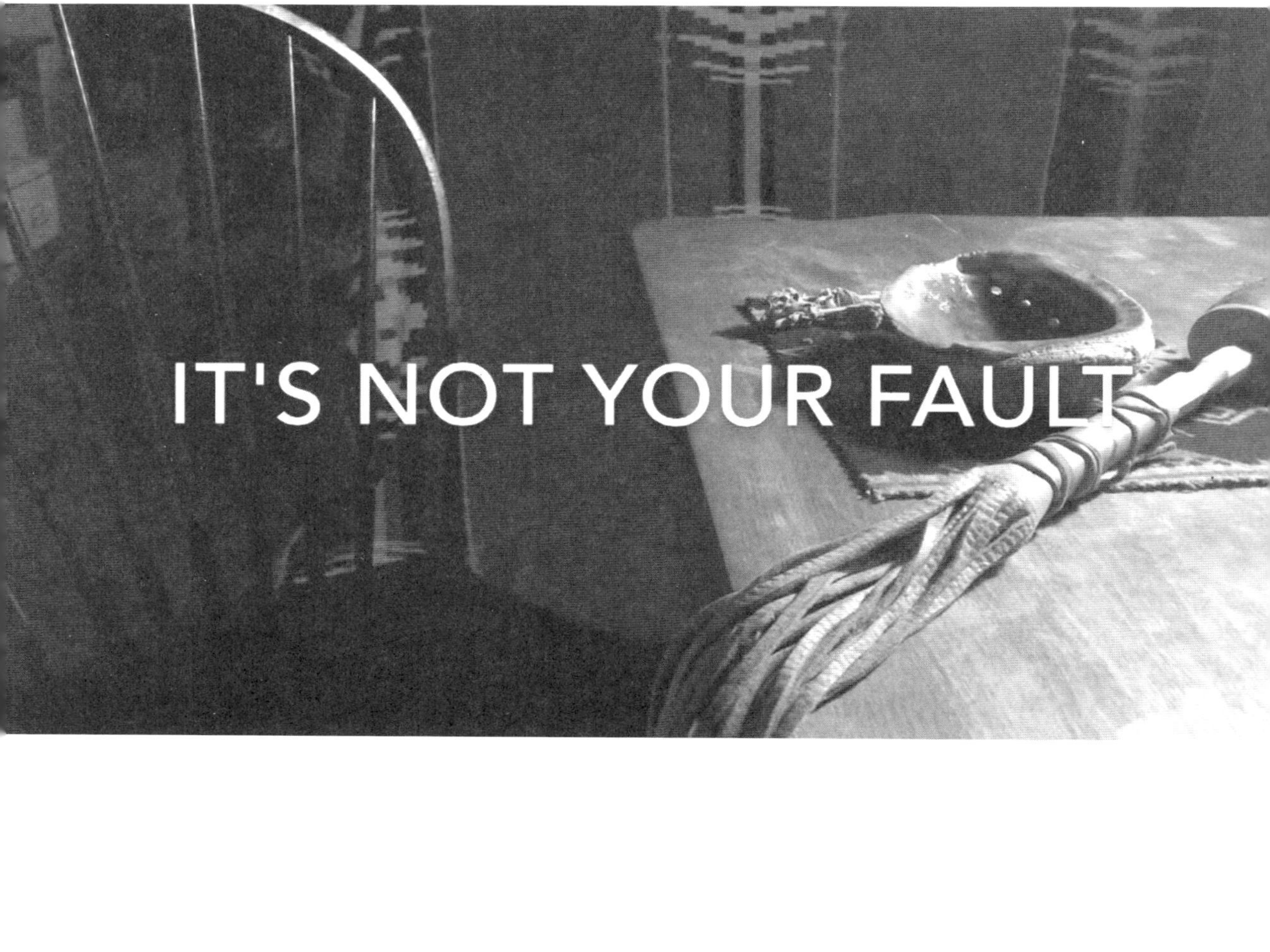
IT'S NOT YOUR FAULT

and murdered women, children, and men associated with these rivers. *Gone But Not Forgotten* (2017) resonated with so many as they stood underneath to reflect on community affected by loss of kin, as it held space for memorialization. With any slight movement from air circulation, the whole structure would move, physically embodying the reverberations felt.

In 2019, I curated an exhibition called Born In Power at the Winnipeg Art Gallery, highlighting Indigenous and Black representation in photography, film, and text, representing acts of reclamation, survivance, and image sovereignty. Black and Indigenous womxn/nonbinary intersectional identities share a collective history of resistance, endurance of intersectional oppression, discrimination, diaspora, sexual violence, and racial objectification/subjugation. Representations of intergenerational Indigenous and Afro/Black bodies were recast, rescripted, and countered by self-determining acts, familial power, and bold vulnerability. Within a dominantly white institutional space, this exhibition posed critiques about sharing marginalized experiences and voices in public, bringing into context the power and privilege of whiteness. What does being born in/born into power mean? Born in Power reflects on the power of photography and film to capture and create constructs of identity and consider the history of photography and media as a colonial tool, an imperial weapon of racial violence and objectification, while witnessing current media exposing ongoing racism and unfathomable violence.[4] In pushing back against these portrayals, and in a gesture toward image sovereignty, Born In Power sought to examine worth, value, and strength in these spaces.

Raven Davis's work *It's Not Your Fault* (2015) is a video and honour song that could be heard faintly throughout the gallery space. Raven Davis affectionally sings the honour song in Anishinaabemowin in a low and consistent chant while sage is lit and burning. Words on the screen describe the NIMMIWG announcement while revealing search engines displaying vulgar race-based violence. It is upsetting and disheartening, but seeing the sage and hearing the persistent song is calming and grounding.

In Kali Spitzer's An Exploration of Resilience and Resistance Project (2015–2020), archival pigment scanned tintypes brilliantly represent BIPOC women and non-binary folks in a vintage tintype portraiture style, while each one of her beautiful subjects tells their stories of resilience on a hidden speaker. Viewers find themselves in a state of awe, peering beyond the image itself to gain a deeper appreciation of experience and insight. With a paracuratorial approach, the exhibition included several community engagement programmatic elements. One program entitled Auntie Lens featured videos of "aunties" from the larger Winnipeg BIPOC community speaking to their experiences and practices of community care. Another program was community tours inviting folks to respond to the exhibition from their perspective and without censorship. Mahlet Cuff created a video interview with Black artists Glodi Bahati and Sappfyre Mcleod about resistance and care. Two MLA powerhouses Nahanni Fontaine and Uzoma Asagwara delivered an online tour of Born In Power to speak to the strength in solidarity as acts of care.

Knowing my mother was my first teacher, listening to her heartbeat and voice in utero, I know I was born in power. Her story was in a way my story, and her fight for justice shared. The gift of life I was given and then to give life as a mother myself—this is power, one to protect and cherish. From my Matriarchal inheritance, I stand in my power in various positionalities in life; curatorial, artistic, with my family and with communities—I strive to amplify Indigenous voices and restore reserves of resilience. Art itself doesn't create change, the people do. Art promotes awareness in various forms and actions, but it's the people challenging systems of oppression, creating collective actions of building awareness and making political changes and policies that are Indigenously self-determined. Reading and listening to the powerful stories of Indigenous women, girls, and 2SLGBTQQIA people about their experiences of gender-based violence in the NIMMIWG helps us understand and fight in power and resistance against Canada's systemic bastion that allows this violence to continue. Can we come to a place and time of recovery, where we recognize and appreciate the mothers of nations, women (womxn), and their power?

[1] Ryan O'Toole, Onyx Sloan Morgan, and Laura McNab-Coombs, "Our Highways, Our Tears: Indigenous Women's and Two Spirit People's Health and Resources Extraction," in *Introduction to Determinants of First Nations, Inuit, and Metis Peoples' Health in Canada*, ed. Margo Greenwood et al. (Toronto: Canadian Scholars, 2022), 103.

[2] The Canadian Encyclopedia, "Indian Act," accessed August 15, 2024, https://www.thecanadianencyclopedia.ca/en/article/indian-act.

[3] "Reducing the number of Indigenous children in care," Government of Canada, https://www.sac-isc.gc.ca/eng/1541187352297/1541187392851.

[4] The Winnipeg Art Gallery, "Born in Power," accessed August 15, 2024, https://www.wag.ca/exhibitions/born-in-power/.

INSURGENCE

Gone But Not Forgotten

CASEY KOYCZAN

Gone But Not Forgotten (2017) pushes for recognition and remembrance of all of the Indigenous people that we have lost over the years in Canada due to the injustices, mistreatment, and economic scrutiny that they face on a daily basis.

The installation is comprised of driftwood I harvested along the banks of the Red River and Assiniboine River in Winnipeg, Manitoba. Numerous bodies have been found within these rivers over the years, and in some form, as the water is all connected, parts of the spirit from the people that have been retrieved from these waters are soaked into the wood and are present with us.

At the end of the Insurgence / Resurgence exhibit, a tour was given to local Manitoba Chiefs and organization leaders to see all of the artworks. After the guide explained my installation's concept and that it would be taken down soon, someone requested to acquire the materials in order to be burned in ceremony. I agreed to this as it was the perfect way to return the spirits and materials to the earth and atmosphere.

Singing Legacy

DEANTHA EDMUNDS

I AM AN ACTOR, writer, composer, teacher, and Canada's first Inuk professional classical singer. I feel blessed to be able to do the work that I do as an artist, and I am grateful for this life each and every day. I believe that everything we do resonates beyond ourselves and out into the world. Singing can be a very powerful tool to connect to yourself and the world around you. When we sing, vibrations move through us and alter our physical being and emotional perspective. Through my work, I aspire for my audience to consider how they view themselves and the people in their lives, how they react to others' stories, and how to move forward with more compassion, acceptance, and love.

In the fall of 2017, I had been reading about and listening to some of the family stories of Missing and Murdered Indigenous Women, Girls, and Two-Spirit people (MMIWG2S) and I became overwhelmed by this genocide. I felt so helpless, so sad. I knew that I had to do something, and the only thing I could think of was to write what I first thought would be a poem—just for me, a personal release. I wanted my words to honour and uplift the voices of those lost. I wrote the lyrics and then the melody of "Legacy." I didn't want it to be a sad song. I wanted to let those lost and stolen sisters know that we will never forget them and we will carry on their love.

This song came from a very personal place, and although I did not have a lot of experience in songwriting at that time, I knew that I needed to put it out into the world and hoped it would somehow make a difference. I had no idea that this song would take me on such an incredible journey, which has still only just begun.

"Legacy" was first shared at a Sisters in Spirit gathering I organized at New Brunswick Community College in Saint John, New Brunswick, where I worked as an Indigenous Advisor in 2017. I sang it a cappella, unaccompanied by any instruments. I hung red dresses around the room in which we gathered, as well as around both campuses in Saint John, with cards explaining Jaime Black-Morsette's REDress Project.

My first performance of "Legacy" in St. John's, Newfoundland and Labrador, was for a virtual concert in May 2021, in the midst of the COVID-19 global pandemic. Leslee Heys, who is an incredible musician and composer in St. John's, arranged and orchestrated my song, and I performed it as soloist with two members of Lady Cove Women's Choir and the Newfoundland Symphony Orchestra. She wrote the oboe part to represent the voices of our lost and stolen sisters, their wandering spirits walking beside me throughout the song. I had the chorus translated into Inuttitut—the dialect of Inuktitut spoken in Nunatsiavut, the ancestral homeland of the Labrador Inuit, where my father grew up. Leslee arranged my song beautifully, and the very last line in Inuttitut means "it's not goodbye."

July 1 is Canada Day, a national holiday, but in 2021, news had just broken about hundreds of Indigenous children lying in unmarked graves at the grounds of the former Kamloops Indian Residential School in British Columbia. Instead of celebrating our country that Canada Day, we held a song-sharing session at a public park in St. John's to honour the missing and murdered Indigenous children. Now we know there are thousands of Indigenous children who died in the residential school system. Hundreds of people were in attendance, and they raised their voices in singing "Legacy" along with me, in harmony, accompanied by stringed instruments played by volunteer musicians from the community. It felt fitting to raise our voices together to acknowledge the children who died at residential schools, to send love out into the world to them and their families, rather than celebrate the country that made that happen and hid it.

In my work, I always appreciate the opportunity to collaborate with other Indigenous artists. In 2022, I was delighted to have Mi'kmaq dancer Sarah Prosper join me on stage during my performance of "Legacy" at One Sky: Artist Showcase, part of the Spirit Song Festival. The Spirit Song Festival is a multi-day event that celebrates Indigenous arts and culture, running every year in St. John's since 2013. While I sang, Sarah danced in a red dress around me, and ten other Indigenous women wearing red joined us silently on stage in a semicircle—the shape of an ulu, the traditional Inuit women's curved knife. The feeling in the performance hall was heavy with emotion, but also there was a sense of quiet strength, solidarity, and warmth. Sarah's beautiful dancing took the significance of my song to a deeper level. As she moved around me and the other women, the breeze she created brought to my mind the energy of MMIWG2S that will never expire. I felt supported by the women surrounding me, and the vibrancy of their red dresses was striking on stage, a familiar and beloved representation of our Lost and Stolen Sisters, thanks to Jaime Black-Morsette's REDress Project.

What's next for me and my song "Legacy"? My dream is to create a music video with a youth choir, an American Sign Language choir, and string quartet with oboe, as a symbol of the younger generation taking up the cause, voicing the message of peace, love, and hope for change, to bring us closer to justice and peace for MMIWG2S. My hope is that it will be carried far and wide on the breath of singers from all walks of life, not only mine.

LEGACY

No matter how long,
How near, how far,
Led by Sister Sun or the North Star,
You will be found,
We'll sing you home,
Your beautiful Spirit not left to roam.

Sister, I feel you walking with me
I hear your voice on the breeze
And I know that you will always be
More than a memory,
Alive like the wind flying free.

You left us a legacy:
Hold on to your history,
Write a new plot,
Dance, drum, do not forget
It's never too late to rise and resonate!

Nukak, ippiniavagit pisuKatigigavit
Tusaavagit anugimmi
Kauijimavunga ullu tamaat
IkKaumanginnaniakKagit
Anugittut tingijuk

We stand with you,
We speak for you.
We hold you high,
It's not goodbye.

Sister, I feel you walking with me
I hear your voice on the breeze
And I know that you will always be
More than a memory,
Alive like the wind flying free.

Atsunaingilagut

Omaeqnomenew

Save Her (Savior)

CRYSTAL LEPSCIER

S*ave Her (Savior)* (2019) was created to invoke the idea that turning to culture can empower our Indigenous daughters to fight the epidemic of Missing and Murdered Indigenous Women, Girls, and Two-Spirit people. This piece features my niece, who attended Menominee culture camp where the image of her with a red handprint over her mouth was taken by a relative. She commonly engages in dancing fancy-shawl style at powwows, and exploring her culture through dancing shows connection to her relationships and responsibility as a Menominee youth. Dancing is one of her sources of strength. The design from the fancy shawl is also repeated in a beadwork pattern on the background of the painting. The colours and design of this beadwork pattern were carefully selected specifically for the wearer and are important elements of representation of my niece.

Red Dresses and Moccasin Vamps

Art, Community Engagement, and Social Change

SHERRY FARRELL RACETTE

This piece is based on a paper presented for the panel "Curating Against Colonialism" presented at Resisting, Reclaiming, Reframing: Indigenous Communities and Art Museum Collections Symposium, International Observatory for Cultural Heritage, Columbia University, New York, March 8, 2019.

ONE OF THE MOST difficult realities confronting Indigenous women globally is the intense violence that results in our extreme vulnerability to sexual assault and murder. There are high numbers of Missing and Murdered Indigenous Women, Girls, and Two-Spirit people (MMIWG2S)—thousands of cases in Canada alone—many unsolved. In 2008, the United Nations called upon the Canadian government to take action and investigate why these "cases have neither been fully investigated nor attracted priority attention, with the perpetrators unpunished."[1] The Committee on the Elimination of Racial Discrimination, which issued the demand, had received a high-profile American delegation from the Indian Law Resource Centre earlier the same year to discuss "the shocking rates of physical and sexual violence against Native women" and the United States government's failure to offer either protection or justice.[2]

In feminist discourse, an attack on women through popular culture and media imagery is called *symbolic annihilation*: the absence, underrepresentation, and distorted representation of a group of people or gender. The strategies of symbolic annihilation described by Gaye Tuchman are: omit, trivialize, and condemn.[3] Whatever police and media attention MMIWG2S cases have received has been profoundly influenced by stereotypical discourse that produces images of Indigenous women as deserving of the violence they experience, resulting in apathetic, self-justified inaction.

Women artists have drawn on these horrific circumstances to create installation and performance art directed primarily toward their own communities, but also the general public to counter that indifference and erasure. Michelle La Flamme has named this "theatrical medicine," describing the artistic use of ritualized naming and performative commemoration to restore victims' humanity and produce spaces for the release of trauma.[4] Two projects in particular have mobilized community engagement, moving the work into public spaces, largely outside of galleries and art institutions.

In 2009, Jaime Black-Morsette attended the Hemispheric Institute of Performance and Politics' Encuentro gathering in Bogotá, Colombia. She witnessed Patricia Ariza's four-hour performance *Where are they? Living Memory. Women in the Public Square,* which involved three hundred women, many of whom were survivors of violence.[5] The image of the red dresses worn by the women stayed with Jaime, who at the time was teaching in The Pas in northern Manitoba, the site of Helen Betty Osborne's murder, a notorious case of secrecy, collusion, and delayed justice. She asked for donations of red dresses to represent the physical forms of missing and murdered women, and launched the REDress Project, installing the first group of red dresses in 2010. In a 2011 interview, she stated that she found "the symbol of the red dress both subtle and compelling and also very, very simple and accessible."[6] Originally conceptualized as a guerrilla action, to be installed at night, she decided that

> it seemed difficult to inform the public what the project was about that way. The main goal of the project is to reach as many people as possible, people who are not necessarily artists, or activists or Aboriginal, so I chose to show the work in publicly accessible spaces, outside of the gallery context... I imagine the dresses taking over public space, streets and parks and trees covered in empty red dresses, until the whole city is mourning the loss of these women, until something is done.[7]

The dresses were primarily installed on university campuses, until in 2014, following the grim discovery of fifteen-year-old Tina Fontaine's body in Winnipeg's Red River, the artist put out a call asking people to hang red dresses in their window, on their balcony, to express visible support for a national inquiry. The same year, a permanent installation was prominent in the new Canadian Museum for Human Rights. The red dress has become one of the most widely recognized symbols of MMIWG2S. It has been taken up by many people, often appearing spontaneously, as individuals enact Black-Morsette's original guerrilla intent, as in the red dresses that appeared overnight along Winnipeg's Red River at the site where Tina Fontaine's body was recovered.

In 2012, a very different project, Walking With Our Sisters (WWOS), was launched by Métis artist Christi Belcourt. Deeply affected by the as yet unsolved disappearance of two girls from Maniwaki, Belcourt envisioned a pathway of moccasin vamps representing each woman's interrupted life. It was a simple premise—that people would walk alongside them and contemplate this profound loss. She contacted artists and created a Facebook page, which became a central point of communication, sharing, and motivation. She asked for beaded moccasin vamps, initially hoping for six hundred—which was then the estimated number of cases. One of the phenomena of the project was the beading circles that sprang up—an estimated sixty-eight community-based groups. Most were in Canada, several in the United States, and one I mentored via Skype in Aberdeen, Scotland. More than one thousand artists contributed vamps, sewn lovingly, often dedicated to much-missed family members and friends. Belcourt ultimately received nearly two thousand pairs of vamps, which uncannily reflected the numbers of MMIWG2S in more recent studies at the time.[8] As the packages began to arrive, first slowly and then in a deluge, she was on first-name terms with every delivery person and Canada Post worker who arrived at her door.

The project has been managed by a National Collective of volunteers led by Belcourt, with each installation organized by local collectives of volunteers, organizations, and Elders. The first installation was in Edmonton, Alberta, in 2013; the final in Batoche, Saskatchewan, in August 2019. Over seven years, WWOS travelled to twenty-four locations in Canada and the United States, installed in community and cultural centres, universities, and small galleries.

WWOS is ponderous and slow, demanding deep community engagement and working with Elders and families. Each community determined the design of the installation and programmed an array of actions and activities to address violence. From the beginning, WWOS has been inclusive. Anyone could submit vamps, anyone could volunteer, all were welcome: church groups, people of all backgrounds, anyone who wanted to express solidarity. The value of this was brought home many times. In Winnipeg, I walked through the installation with a father, still grieving the loss of his daughter after many years. It meant so much to him that people from "all walks of life" cared enough to create a pair of vamps. Each stitch reflected love and care.

Fundraising, supporting, and programming each community site required dozens of volunteers, and planning began months before "the Sisters" arrived. It took days to install and pack up. The installation had to be fully supported at all times, as people who came to walk with the sisters experienced grief, shock, and anger. The beauty of the installation and kindness of volunteers and venue staff were palpable counterbalances. Activities opened spaces to work through feelings and share tough stories. Stitching became an important continuing action. People kept beading and they beaded together. Volunteers drove "the bundle," as it was lovingly called, to the next location. These were often long, exhausting drives. In Winnipeg, we welcomed organizers from Parry Sound with a feast. From Akwesasne it went to North Battleford. From Saskatoon, volunteers drove to Yellowknife. In December!

Installing was particularly difficult work. Written on the back of the beautiful surfaces of the vamps are heartfelt dedications: "Miss you," "Love you Mom." Ceremony was an important, and occasionally controversial, aspect of Walking With Our Sisters. At Urban Shaman, we almost lost our lease due to complaints about smudging from other tenants in the building. Negotiating our spiritually diverse communities and the wide range of cultural protocols was challenging. Overzealous participants occasionally enforced, rather than offered, choices to wear a skirt, smudge, or carry tobacco. Many were grieving family members. Emotions were always close to the surface.

There were also beautiful surprises: spontaneous musical performances, gifts of a buffalo skull, Eagle staffs, drums, and the tobacco laid down by young men. In Regina, students at a local high school completed their vamps, installed them in their school, and organized a community symposium. In Whitehorse, comfort shawls were made by the host committee and gifted to the project. In Sault Ste. Marie, WWOS was installed in the old Shingwauk Residential School, and the resident Elders group put out a call for small vamps representing children who died at residential schools. They are a heartbreaking group of 107 tiny vamps.

The project resonates long after "the Sisters" travel on. A group of men from a high security prison outside Winnipeg followed the project on social media and spoke about their own experiences as both perpetrators and victims of violence. Unable to walk through the installation, they made a star blanket and gifted it to the director of Urban Shaman, who joined their talking circle as one of WWOS Winnipeg's outreach activities. Community relationships forged during WWOS have had the capacity to regroup to address new challenges.

Several important artistic projects preceded REDress and WWOS. Rebecca Belmore's seminal performance and installation works, *Vigil* and *The Named and the Unnamed*, were organized in conjunction with Vancouver's 2002 Talking Stick Festival. These were visceral responses to the women who disappeared from Vancouver's Downtown Eastside. Belmore shouted names and pulled roses through her mouth in painful gestures of memory. Dressed in red, she nailed her dress to a pole and struggled to tear herself free.[9] Also in 2002, Montreal-based Claudia Bernal created *Monument to Ciudad Juarez: Only Women Who Died a Violent Death Go to Heaven*, an ephemeral monument, which in various iterations included concentric circles of candles, ceramic containers, fabric, stone, and a video projection.[10] Lesser known but also important was the 2006 *Give Her a Face* by Saskatchewan artists Joi Arcand, Felicia Gay, and Chrystal Kruszelnicki at Grunt Gallery in Vancouver. The artists dedicated the exhibition to Calinda Waterhen (age 22), Shelly Napope (age 16), Eva Taysup (age 25), Mary Jane Serloin (age 35), Janet Sylvestre (age 37), and Shirley Lonethunder (age 26)—all victims of the same serial murderer. Enacted and documented in Saskatoon, the artists put themselves in the space of the women, literally wrapping themselves in blankets as the bodies had been when discovered, and lying in the same locations. This action echoed the women who attended the trial wrapped in blankets in solidarity with the victims. In their collective artist statement the artists declared they "believe it is only through our collective silence that issues such as these go unnoticed and unchallenged."[11] In addition to the aforementioned *Women in the Public Square* (2009), *Los Zapatos Rojos (The Red Shoes)* by Elina Chauvet was first installed in Juarez, Mexico, in 2009.[12] A changing installation ranging from dozens to hundreds of red shoes, it travelled for eight years, asserting the presence of missing and murdered women in multiple urban centres.

Artists have countered symbolic annihilation with powerful, symbolic representation, but violence against Indigenous women continues at an alarming rate. They have broken the silence, and through community engagement have had a significant role in the long-lobbied-for, but ultimately disappointing, National Inquiry into Missing and Murdered Indigenous Women and Girls (2016–2019), but we are now at a critical point. Visual imagery, no matter how powerful, can only create spaces of dialogue, making the "unnamed" visible, resisting erasure. Solutions must come from systemic action and change. However, as long as we struggle for basic safety, the REDress Project in particular continues to bring energy and focus to important anti-violence movements.

In *Vigil* and *Give Her a Face*, the female face and body were embraced in artistic action. In 2017, Cree dancer Tia Wood sponsored the Healing of the Red Dress Special at the Gathering of Nations powwow in Albuquerque.[13] As head woman dancer, Wood used the platform to organize a jingle dress "special" inspired by Black-Morsette's REDress installations in public spaces, this time with vibrant, living bodies in red dresses. Images and videos flooded multiple social media sites. It has since been taken up by other dancers. By now, hundreds of women have worn red, dancing to honour MMIWG2S and declare their own vulnerability. Taos designer Patricia Michaels closed the 2019 Santa Fe Indian Art Market Haute Couture Fashion show with a group of women singers standing in formation at the base of the stage, while solemn women in red walked the runway as images and statistics were projected on a screen.[14] The models included a slight white-haired Elder, and finally two young girls. It was profoundly moving.

A recent project, Red Shawl/Sacred MMIWG, a series of portraits by Anishinaabe photographer Nadya Kwandibens, evolved out of the National Inquiry and focuses on family members, who are the living victims.[15] Here, a son with his mother's photograph and a sister who has organized two memorial marches a year for decades. The tireless activism and endless mourning of children, parents, brothers, and sisters can sometimes be lost.

There is no doubt these projects have had enormous impact on public awareness, have shifted government policies, given voice to Indigenous women, and created space for critically important conversations. In 2023, the Search The Landfill campaign deployed the red dress to draw attention to the heartbreaking and frustrated efforts of families calling for a search of Winnipeg landfills to locate the remains of at least two women, Morgan Harris and Marcedes Myran, victims of a serial killer.[16] Red dresses have been painted on streets and carried at demonstrations; and 101 red dresses, including one over three metres in length, were hung on the chain-link fence at Winnipeg's Brady landfill. They are still there. Creating, installing, and bringing dresses have been a means to express support for the brave actions of Cambria Harris, the young daughter who is spearheading a movement. The red dresses of Search The Landfill illustrate the ways a symbol can give voice and courage, and, ideally, mobilize political action toward the change we seek.[17]

[1] David Mutimer, *Canadian Annual Review of Politics and Public Affairs 2008* (University of Toronto Press, 2015), 107.

[2] For an overview see "Ending Violence Against Native Women," *Indian Law Resource Center*, https://indianlaw.org/issue/ending-violence-against-native-women.

[3] Gaye Tuchman, "The Symbolic Annihilation of Women by the Mass Media," in *Culture and Politics*, ed. Crothers and Lockhart (Palgrave Macmillan, 2000): 150–74.

[4] Michelle La Flamme, "Theatrical Medicine: Aboriginal Performance, Ritual and Commemoration (for Vanessa Lee Buckner)," *TRiC/RTaC* 32, no. 2 (2010): 107–17.

[5] For documentation of the performance see "Patricia Ariza: Where are they? Living Memory. Women in the Public Square," Hemispheric Institute of Performance and Politics, Encuentro Archive, August 27, 2009, https://hemisphericinstitute.org/en/enc09-urban-interventions/item/121-09-patricia-ariza.html.

[6] "About the REDress Project," Indigenous Foundations, First Nations and Indigenous Studies, University of British Columbia, 2009, http://indigenousfoundations.arts.ubc.ca/about_the_redress_project/.

[7] Ibid.

[8] Maryanne Pearce, "An Awkward Silence: Missing and Murdered Vulnerable Women and the Canadian Justice System," PhD dissertation, University of Ottawa, 2013.

[9] Maggie Tate, "Re-presenting Invisibility: Ghostly Aesthetics in Rebecca Belmore's *Vigil* and *The Named and the Unnamed*," *Visual Studies* 30, no. 1 (2015): 20–31.

[10] Mariette Bouillet, "Claudia Bernal: monument à Ciudad Juárez," *Inter* 91 (Fall 2005): 52–55; Natalie Alvarez, "Latina Performance North and Transnational *Acciones* Against Feminicide in the Americas," in *Theatre and Cartographies of Power: Repositioning the Latina/o Americas*, ed. Noriega and Santana (Southern Illinois University Press, 2018): 249–63.

[11] "Give Her a Face: Joi Arcand, Felicia Gay & Chrystal Kruszelnicki," *Brunt Magazine online*, no. 3, Grunt Gallery, Vancouver, http://bruntmag.com/issue3/give-her-a-face.html.

[12] This project has had multiple iterations and travelled internationally. Ruth Trinidad Galván, "Collective Memory of Violence of the Female Brown Body: A Decolonial Feminist Public Pedagogy Engagement with the Feminicides," *Pedagogy, Culture & Society* 24, no. 3 (2016): 343–57.

[13] Jeremy Harpe interview with Tia Wood, "'Shocked and Honored' Says Young Powwow Dancer," *Windspeaker*, April 26, 2017, https://windspeaker.com/news/windspeaker-news/shocked-and-honored-says-young-powwow-dancer.

[14] Patricia Michaels, Haute Couture Fashion Show, SWAIA Indian Market (Southwestern Association for Indian Arts), Santa Fe, New Mexico, August 18, 2019.

[15] The campaign also included advocates and survivors of violence. See SacredMMIWG / FFADAsacrées (@sacred_mmiwg), https://www.instagram.com/sacred_mmiwg/.

[16] The remains of serial killer victims are believed to be in Winnipeg landfills, as other victims had been found in city dumpsters. See Bruce Hoye, "Group Hangs 101 Red Dresses Outside Winnipeg Landfill as Calls for Search of Human Remains Continue," *CBC News*, January 15, 2023, https://www.cbc.ca/news/canada/manitoba/brady-landfill-mmiwg-search-red-dresses-1.6714973.

[17] In January 2024, Morgan Harris's family brought two human rights complaints against the Progressive Conservative party for using opposition to the landfill campaign in election ads and the current government for inaction. Charles Lefebvre, "Family of Homicide Victim Files Human Rights Complaints over Manitoba Election Ads, Lack of Landfill Search," *CTV News*, January 16, 2024, https://winnipeg.ctvnews.ca/family-of-homicide-victim-files-human-rights-complaints-over-manitoba-election-ads-lack-of-landfill-search-1.6728661.

SHE HOLDS
WATER

The water in me,
recognizes you.

— JAIME BLACK-MORSETTE

Ishkode. Noodin. Aki. Nibi.
Ishkode. Noodin. Aki. Nibi.
Ishkode. Noodin. Aki. Nibi.

Nibi. Nibi. Nibi. Nibi.

THE DRINK

When I was little I remember my grandpa calling the lake "the drink." And we did, he would dip a cup in the lake and take a long drink then pass the cup to us. It seemed like every time we were with him we were on the water in his old outboard boat he painted red. We would leave camp mornings when the mist was on the lake and the sun hadn't quite come over the horizon and we wouldn't come back until late. Cooler full of lake trout and sometimes pickerel for dinner. When we were out on the water everyone was happy. In between fishing I was allowed to jump into the lake to swim. At first when I was three or four, my mom would tie my lifejacket to the boat so I wouldn't go too far, and later I would dive as deep as I possibly could into the over three hundred feet of water of Sturgeon Lake. Under the surface there was no sound except the sound of my own heartbeat. I would always open my eyes and watch how the light spilled and refracted through the water, how the sun made a halo of light that I would follow back up to the surface.

let me slip between worlds
the place we came from
liquid stars

suspended mercurial

shifting shapes
loosening into waves
the quickening of a current
moved by moon

WATER CARRIER

A few months before I become pregnant with my son I am looking through maps; maps of waterways, historical maps, the Selkirk Treaty, a hand-drawn map of the Red River with the marks of the chiefs. The treaty was never intended to cede or surrender the land but to live alongside each other on the land.

I find the map of the waterways that were followed as trade routes between Thunder Bay and the Red River basin, a map of the Great Lakes. I burn these images onto a printing screen and begin printing them in red ink onto images of my own body. The river systems become my veins, a network of blood moving through me.

I print the image of Lake Winnipeg in red overlaid onto a black and white photo of my womb; this is the water that I carry, the history of these waters will live and be passed on through me to the next generation. I am thinking on how to hold these waters, how to care for this history, what to release and what to hold on to. How to embody presence and power, to reclaim and retell our history of resistance and resilience in the face of ongoing efforts to seize control over our lands and our bodies.

WATER WALKER

I join the water walk at Selkirk, just outside of Winnipeg, quickly changing into my red dress and racing out to meet the walkers. A clutch of women in ribbon skirts, an Eagle staff tied with 134 Red Ribbons, to represent the 134 women who have been found lifeless in the Red River. The women take turns carrying a copper vessel filled with water from the very beginning of the walk, over five hundred miles south of here. Sharon Day has gathered the walkers and led them in this fifty-three-day ceremony. We walk in prayer, in reverence for the water and for the women.

There are teachings that we women are water carriers, water protectors. That we hold the waters of creation within our bodies, and that all human life comes from that original water within us.

Our bodies are made of water and that water holds memory. I think about all the water on this earth and how it is the same water that flowed millions of years ago, the same water that our ancestors and their ancestors drank and cleaned and swam in. That the water in me is connected to the water in you and is the source of all life.

WATER SONG[1]

Wishit-ta do ya, do ya, do ya
Wishi-ta do ya, do ya hay
Wishi-ta do ya, do ya, do ya
Wishi-ta do ya do ya hay

Wish a ta nay a hay a hay a
Wish a ta nay a hay a hay
Wish a ta nay a hay a hay a
Wish a ta nay a haya hay

This is a water song. Women carry the responsibility of caring for the water. We sing it slowly the first time through, faster the second time, and faster again on the third time. On the fourth time through, we sing it slowly again without drumming. Water moves, sometimes fast, sometimes slow.

Bev Williamson taught us this song.

[1] Linda Beacham, *Maang Gonaandaagozid*, 4th ed. (2017).

Untitled

JAIME BLACK-MORSETTE

cheek to loam
a living network of green
pressed along the pathway
from hip to heart
the water in me recognizes you
knows the rush
and the slow
emergence
unfolding from dark
earth
sending out roots
like fingertips
feeling for home

The Four Elements

KC ADAMS

NIBI (WATER) is life; without nibi, we cannot survive. Nibi is the sacred thread that binds all creation. Its presence transforms the essence of our landscapes, breathing life upon the earth's surface. From the gentle babbling brooks to the vast, boundless oceans, nibi precipitates stories of renewal and rebirth, infusing every living creature with the essence of vitality.

Nibi is our relative.
Nibi is a part of us.

Nibi starts the circle.

In the rich tapestry of my Anishinaabe heritage, women are revered as water carriers and water protectors, for within our bodies we take on a new life via the sustentation of nibi.[1] As we journey through the sacred path of motherhood, we become vessels of nourishment, cradling our children within the gentle embrace of embryonic waters. Esteemed Knowledge Keepers like Maria Campbell illuminate the profound significance of nibi as a conduit between the spiritual realm and earthly existence.[2] Within the depths of this flowing connection, women, with their capacity to harbour life's essence, impart the spirit of nibi to their offspring, bestowing them the gift of life. Thus, in recognition of this intimate bond with nibi, women are tasked with caring for and protecting this vital relative that supports all living beings.

As I gaze upon the ancient clay vessels formed by my Indigenous ancestors, I feel the presence of the ancestor's nibi responsibility from the very core of the containers' forms and adornments. With their rounded shapes that extend to the bottom, these clay pots echo the sacred swell of pregnancy, a testament to the nurturing spirit of our female ancestors. Etched upon their rims, intricate patterns reminiscent of umbilical twists speak to the enduring bond between mother and child.[3] At the same time, the delicate punctuations remind me of our Grandmother Moon, casting her luminous gaze and influence on our oceans and bodies. As I study these intricate designs, I can't help but feel a deep respect for the importance of nibi in their lives. It's like our ancestors left us a message in the patterns and shapes of these clay pots, reminding us of how essential nibi is to everything we do, from birth to growth to sustaining life itself.

As I embark upon sculpting my own clay vessel, I am acutely aware of the profound presence of nibi intricately woven into the very fabric of its creation. Nibi, with its formidable presence, flows over rocks, yielding microparticles that traverse the waters, eventually settling along the riverbanks to form clay beds. It is here that I find myself, amidst the quiet reverence of the aki (earth/land), seeking clay infused with the essence of nibi's influence, ever mindful of offering my respects and honouring the teachings of reciprocity. This is where I feel in touch with my female ancestors, imagining them collecting clay in the same way.

Should the clay be dry, I introduce nibi, which expands the clay like a sponge and is rendered pliable and receptive to my touch. As I shape each coil of clay, I'm constructing a tribute to the women who bring life into the world. It's my way of honouring the knowledge passed down by my ancestors, who held water in sacred reverence as its guardians.

As I bagidanaamowin (breathe out), tiny droplets of water vapour escape into the air. When I am shaping the clay pot, my breath becomes part of the mix, blending with the material and becoming a subtle part of the vessel itself.[4] As I shape and mould the clay, infusing it with the essence of my being, the ambient warmth of the surroundings causes nibi to evaporate, ascending into the clouds as tiny droplets, continuing its timeless journey of nourishment and sustenance.

When nibi has departed from the vessel, leaving only echoes of its presence, ishkode (fire) is introduced, breathing life into the clay body. In this sacred alchemy of transformation, men, as integral community members, tend to the flames, supporting and safeguarding the vessels as they undergo their metamorphosis. Just as Indigenous men in the past would honour their role in protecting and uplifting women, they would nurture the pots within the fire, ensuring they emerge as vessels of life-giving nourishment for the community. Each pot is a testament to the enduring bond between humanity and the sacred waters that sustain us all.

Nibi is life.

Nibi is everywhere.
Nibi continues the circle.

[1] Bethany Helaine Poltl, "What Does Water Mean to You?" *Imprint,* April 11, 2024, https://uwimprint.ca/article/what-does-water-mean-to-you/.

[2] Kim Anderson, "Aboriginal Women, Water and Health: Reflections from Eleven First Nations, Inuit, and Métis Grandmothers," *Prairie Women's Health Centre of Excellence*, October 2010, http://www.pwhce.ca/womenAndWater.htm.

[3] As explained by Kevin Brownlee at the Manitoba Museum, January 23, 2020.

[4] The four elements are part of the clay-making process including our breath, as taught by Gordie (Wolf Child) and Madeline Walker in conversation on September 2, 2023, at Misipawistik's Annual Women's Gathering, Grand Rapids, Manitoba.

Holding Space Between Here and the Sky

JENNIFER LEE SMITH

I OFTEN WONDER HOW love overcomes grief, how we can remain hopeful in a world that holds cruelty in it. I wish with all my heart that it did not exist. How do we continue holding space for love and community? How do we care for each other?

The Indigenous women I get to walk alongside in this world are everything to me; they are a grounding force keeping me close to the earth and each other, and they are also a celestial force that makes me feel like anything is possible when we are together. We are the connection between the earth and the skies. This is the place where the cycles of love and relationship can exist in an infinite relationship. A relationship like the cycles of the earth that grows and provides and nurtures.

Through their performances, artists KC Adams and Jaime Black-Morsette hold space that is grounded and physical while also extremely spiritual. Their performance *they tried to bury us* brought together the elements of fire, air, earth, and water into a space where KC and Jaime interacted with them through ritual and ceremony.

In the centre of the room was a clay vessel, with rocks and a hide placed near it. KC and Jaime entered the room and began interacting with the objects and each other, moving through a cycle of washing the rocks or dribbling water onto them, handing them to each other, placing them on each other's bodies, holding the rocks, and covering each other in the hide and the rocks.

At times the projections on the wall were interrupted by the ways KC and Jaime moved their bodies around the space, looking as if smoke was rising from their hands, or that their bodies were moving into the images, which felt like they were moving beyond the physical space we were in.

The elements were always present.

Fire was seen through moving images projected on the wall showing the flames of a wood fire, medicines being burned, and the smoke rising into the air. Air surrounded us as it always does but was made visible through the smoke projected on the walls, and audible through KC and Jaime's interactions and the breaths they were taking that seemed like a form of communication with each other. Earth was brought into the room through rocks and clay vessels they passed to each other and interacted with. Water was held in the clay vessels; the rocks were washed in the water.

The performance focused on exchange between KC and Jaime and cycles. Through the water and the rock there was ancient knowledge in the room that held histories we can never know, but have lived in the past, are still present with us now, and will be here in the future. They are an archive that holds our stories that can only be accessed through building a relationship with them and understanding their presence outside of a narrative story. The water, rocks, clay vessel, and hide were all part of the lands the performance was on, the lands both KC and Jaime's ancestors lived on, and the lands they live on today. This is also a cycle of knowledge and relationship that holds deep meaning.

The title of the performance holds the idea of these cycles and their continuation. *they tried to bury us* implies a trauma that was meant to break the cycle, that burying is a form of hiding something or throwing it away. But the soil is also where life comes from; burying something living does not mean it will not rise and thrive again. Burying seeds and bulbs is a part of a constant cycle of life that needs intervention to stop, but even intervention cannot always stop the rebirth.

Cycles, growth, birth, and rebirth are similar connections to those that Indigenous women build together. KC and Jaime's performances include the deep connections they feel and are building together. They embody a constant earthly presence while engaging with something we cannot see with our eyes, but that we can feel. During their performance of *they tried to bury us,* it was clear that the audience was separate from KC and Jaime and that we were getting to witness interactions that were not our own. Rather, we were being invited into these interactions through the visual representations, and if we were open to it, we could also receive the emotional gift of the performance.

I have also been present for other performances KC and Jaime have come together for. I personally felt both a part of what was happening and separate. I could feel connections to ideas of community and culture that I explore through my own curatorial practice. I felt like they were inviting me into their world within the performance, and I was welcome to be present and engage deeply with what was going on, but that there was also something special happening. It was only possible for the two women working to understand their relationship to each other and how that plays a role both here on earth and in the cosmos outside of our earthly bodies.

In past performances by KC and Jaime, they have either entirely been outside or have moved between indoor and outdoor spaces. *they tried to bury us* was completely inside, and elements of the natural world were brought indoors for the performance. The space was dark, with black walls and very little lighting, taking away all distractions besides the projections, KC, Jaime, and the materials they brought into the space. This is sharply different from experiencing a performance in a busy gallery setting, or on the banks of a river as past performances of theirs have been.

Each of these venues have benefits of their own. For context, the performance in a busy gallery setting was for the exhibition *Shards* at the University of Winnipeg's Gallery 1C03. This performance started inside the gallery and eventually moved out of the gallery into a grassy area of the university facing out onto a busy street. Jaime physically moved from being in a plexiglass case on display in the gallery, to being let free, to moving with KC outside and engaging with clay, the land, and each other. The movement between the gallery display case to the outside referenced what our material culture that is held in galleries might feel like if it was taken out of collection rooms or off of display and let back out onto the lands it is from—lands that are vastly altered by large buildings and traffic—and on a small plot of grass that is a reminder of the land beneath the city.

The performance KC and Jaime did for the exhibition *níchiwamiskwém | nimidet | my sister*, performed on the banks of the St. Lawrence River in Tiohtià:ke/Montreal, honoured the lands and waterways they were guests on. Those who gathered around them to watch the performance were handed small clay vessels or shards of clay vessels to hold during the performance. Those gathered sat on the ground on a small hill looking down on the performance while birds flew overhead and children ran around the grounds. The life of our planet was all around us while the water flowed by on its continuous path behind KC and Jaime.

In contrast, the dark room of *they tried to bury us* served as a place of awakening, where KC and Jaime slowly rose and moved around each other; they were in orbit of one another. From their perspective as performers, there were things around them: an audience, the building structure, and so on, but there was a line where the audience stopped and it was only their space. The wall the audience faced held the projections, but in many ways the wall dissolved and became a portal. This portal may have served many purposes—it could have been a connection to an ancestral realm; a portal that allowed them to break down the barriers of the building around them and allow us to feel less contained; or a portal to the light as the life in them was rejuvenated from the dark.

Being buried does not mean the end, it is a cycle of rest and life. Connections through rhizomes and roots hold us together until we reach for the light and vibrant new beginnings. Our relationships to each other and the ways we foster them can hold the grief, can help us thrive, and can be the light we need to grow.

Sacred Stones in Whiteshell Evidence of Matrilineal Societies

DIANE MAYTWAYASHING

MY SPIRIT NAME IS YELLOW SUN WOMAN, and I am from the Bald Eagle Clan. My other name is Diane Maytwayashing. I am an Anishinaabe woman, with Scottish ancestry, a mother, grandmother, great-grandmother, and in a partnership with a gentle-hearted man. I'm a Knowledge Keeper of the sacred stones in the Whiteshell, a women's pipe carrier, a veteran sun dancer, keeper of a madoodison and jiisakaan. My family and I live in the small town of Seven Sisters Falls, which is situated outside the Whiteshell Provincial Park, near the site of the sacred stones known as the Whiteshell Petroforms, or Bannock Point Petroforms.

My story of how I became a Knowledge Keeper of these sacred stones is not a romantic story, but rather finding my way to the sacred stone site and learning their knowledge came at a time when I was in a dark depression and deep grief.

My friend suggested we take a drive to Whiteshell Park, a day trip to visit a special place. I didn't know it then, but this place would forever change my life. In other words, this place gave me a deeply spiritual life, a life of purpose and meaning.

This sacred place is known to Anishinaabe people as Manitouabee, meaning "Where The Spirit Sits"; an area where stones were set up hundreds of years ago by my Indigenous ancestors. These stones are set up into various shapes of turtles, water serpents, thunderbird, and sacred women beings—Sky Woman, Spider Woman, and a woman giving birth. The Anishinaabe people say that these stone formations align with the star constellations, and for this reason it is the stars that gave the people these instructions of how life must be lived and how to live on the Earth.

My heart was captivated by the mystery of this deeply spiritual place; it was how I felt on my very first visit nearly thirty years ago. Never had I ever imagined that a place like this existed on our Earth. It was a powerful feeling—as though I were stepping into another dimension. This special place forever changed my life. It felt as though I stood at the gateway to a Great Spiritual Domain, and that is just what happened that day. I stepped into a Spiritual Domain on a physical and spiritual level.

That day, my friend Leonard Martin, who brought me to this sacred stone site, had also given me the gift of meaning and life purpose by sharing with me his knowledge of these sacred stones. He respectfully gave credit for this acquired knowledge of the petroforms to his Elder and teacher, the late Peter O'Cheise.

Nearly three decades have passed since I first walked through the sacred stone site, and since that time I have spent eleven consecutive years participating in vision quests for healing, knowledge, and guidance from these stones. This place had revived and healed my life on many levels, and in return for this legacy, it became known to me that it was my responsibility to share this knowledge with the people. Importantly, I felt this responsibility to protect the sacred stones.

These stones are documents and evidence that clearly indicate the history of our Indigenous Matrilineal societies we once had pre-colonization. The stone formations give us this knowledge of this once great reverence Indigenous people held for the women. We see this in the stone formations of the mother giving birth to a baby, in Sky Woman our Creator Goddess—the woman who came down from the stars and created Turtle Island, the continent known as the Americas.

It has been five years that I have been conducting land-based educational tours of the stones in Whiteshell Park, sharing this knowledge with schools, organizations, groups, and families. As time goes by, I really feel that I continue to learn more about the meaning of each stone formation, and for me they are alive and they all have a spirit.

From my knowing, these stones are energy; not only are they alive, but they continue to give us knowledge by teaching us the meaning of life on Mother Earth.

The more we learn about them and make our offerings of tobacco, water, and berries to these stones, we will connect more deeply with their spirit and our spirit. We begin to understand our place on Mother Earth and in the Universe.

This stone site is just one of many sites throughout eastern Manitoba, including the Pimachiowin Aki World Heritage Site located northeast of Manitoba—this site has stones shaped into a moon that would indicate past Matrilineal societies. According to our true Anishinaabe women teachings, time is Matrilineal. We follow the schedule of Mother Earth's four seasonal phases and Grandmother Moon's phases of thirteen moon months. These four seasons are the natural cycles of our land on Turtle Island; these seasons are spring equinox, summer solstice, fall equinox, and winter solstice.

It is during these times of seasonal change where there is an earth and sky spiritual power, and in these seasonal changes Indigenous people will gather in ceremonies with sacred fires and feasts to honour and give gratitude to those spiritual powers of Mother Earth and the Universe.

There are many turtle stone formations in various sizes throughout the Whiteshell. These turtle formations are acknowledged as the keepers of time. The turtle is our living calendar. A turtle's shell consists of thirteen large plates representing thirteen moons on its back with twenty-eight platelets around the outer part of its shell. This would indicate a full moon every twenty-eight days. They are one of the oldest living creatures on Earth, which is also evidence of ancient Matrilineal societies. Together, the turtle and moon work with the natural cycles in time keeping. This is why time is Matrilineal.

The present-day twelve-month Gregorian calendar is used widely around the world, but it is inaccurate when working with the natural cycles of the turtle, moon, and Earth. This inaccuracy is seen in the month of February, where they came up with this concept of a leap year, adding and subtracting days each year. However, this was a way to remove the thirteenth moon in the four seasons. There is no such thing as a blue moon—this is inaccurate in the natural world, but it was a solution for this error of having two moons in one month.

The church took out the thirteenth moon to diminish the sacredness of women and our relationship with the moon. Women are biologically and spiritually connected to the moon, water, and Earth. The number thirteen is a number which represents the sacred feminine. A woman's body corresponds with the rhythms of the moon phases. She will have thirteen menstrual cycles in a four-season year.

Women will give birth during the phases of a full moon or new moon. This is nature. This is a natural power of women.

The stone formation of a woman giving birth in the Whiteshell would be the place of women sharing knowledge of childbirth, menstrual cycles, and women's relationship with the moon and water. For thousands of years, Indigenous women would share moon knowledge at these stones—these teachings would be in reference to how the full moon and new moon affect the waters on Mother Earth, and the spiritual and biological bond between the moon and women.

We all commonly know that we are water, maybe 70 to 90 percent; this is a science. It is during phases of full moon and new moon that the waters on Mother Earth will move. Since we are water, we as well will move during a full moon and new moon. Our emotions will move, our creativity will move, and we feel this heightened energy during a full moon. The Indigenous grandmothers always knew our Grandmother Moon governed all waters on Mother Earth.

These stones are ancient reminders of how we are to live in balance with the natural world, to understand the web of life, to know every living thing is connected in the ecological structures of Mother Earth. The stone shape of a spider teaches us about the complexity of the ecological structures—we call this stone formation Grandmother Spider. The stones give confirmation of the way Indigenous people once lived in complete balance with the natural world.

The knowledge of these stones and their formations confirms this truth of ancient Indigenous Matrilineal tribes' existence for thousands of years. It is possible the stone formations throughout eastern Manitoba could be the last ancient sacred sites on this continent with evidence of the existence of past Matrilineal tribes. It appears perhaps some Knowledge Keepers are shy about pointing out that these stones at Manitouabee are actual evidence of these past Matrilineal societies. We must reclaim the truth. By reclaiming the truth of the knowledge of this sacred site we reclaim our power as Indigenous women, and we stand in that power on our Ancestral homeland.

It's important to mention, this sacred stone site continues to be desecrated—stones are removed and some broken, but another form of desecration is misinterpretation of these sacred stones by archaeology and conservation. These hundreds of stone formations are Knowledge Keepers. They are teachers of the past, giving us knowledge of how Indigenous people thrived for thousands of years on this continent, and the sacredness and deep reverence Indigenous people had for the women.

On Turtle Island, Indigenous women hid the knowledge when it was made illegal to practise ceremonies. Today, Indigenous women carry the knowledge of moon ceremonies and women's teachings. They still have this understanding of Matrilineal ways, and the stones at Manitouabee hold this knowledge of the sacred woman.

It was here at the sacred site, Manitouabee, where I was given the women's pipe to share teachings of the Indigenous Matrilineal ways, and to share the meaning and understanding of how these stones teach us this. It was here where I understood my sacredness as a woman, and an inner spiritual connection to the land. Indigenous Matrilineal knowledge is really about our relationship with the stones, trees, waters, animals, and birds, and knowing they are our relatives.

We cannot learn about Indigenous Matrilineal knowledge in a classroom or conference room. We learn and understand our sacredness as a woman when we are on the lands and in the waters, connecting to and feeling our Mother Earth on a deeply emotional and spiritual level, and we do this by gathering in circles on Mother Earth under Grandmother Moon. This is the true Indigenous Matrilineal way.

RECONCILIATION

Beginning Again

JAIME BLACK-MORSETTE

HERE THE WATER MOVES FAST, we have been coming back to it now for years, so clean you can dip a cup in and take a drink. Here where the prairie turns to rock and bush and climbing the cliff behind camp feels like climbing onto the turtle's back. They say this is where Sky Woman landed when she came from the sky world. Here the stones were placed to mirror the constellations, thousands of years ago.

When she came through the hole in the sky there was no earth, only water. I imagine her there surrounded by the animals taking council, deciding what to do. Then Fisher, diving so deep and deeper still until his paw touched land just as he lost all his air. Fisher slowly rising back up to the surface with his paw still clutched tight around that first piece of land. And all the animals rejoice and mourn Fisher's sacrifice, then gently gift the land into the palm of Sky Woman.

On the bank of the river there are still shards of pottery from the time when our ancestors would come together to create vessels to carry the water, over eight thousand years ago.

And that's what we're doing today. We shape clay into small bowls, our thumbs pressing into the red earth leaving the imprint of our touch. We use water to smooth the edges and the men and boys gather wood for the fire. We leave the bowls to air-dry through the night, and the next day the whole camp gathers around the pit where we will fire the vessels. My son and another young boy are called on and together they light the fire.

SKYWOMAN

they say she came down lightly, made of light but
heavy with it
constellations of memory
a star in the palm
a palm creased with grit
pressing hot earth
over seeds
singing to life
something waiting

SKYWOMAN I

hot visions
a flash of red
coming down from stars

all these stars in the palms
stars in the corners of the eyes
a trail of stars
by the rivers hip
along the shoulder
of the road
in the velvet dark
catching the eye

crumbs of light, heat
step towards
move forward

Image Credits

Page ii–iii
"Women in red dresses in field"
Photograph
Featuring from left to right: Natu Bearwolf, Tiffany Joseph, Erynne Gilpin, Keilah Lukenbill-Williams, Lindsay Delaronde
Photo Credit UATE

Page v
the water in me, recognizes you
2022
Performance still
Artist Jaime Black-Morsette
Photo Credit NK

Page xix
"REDress Project Art Workshop student work, St. Catherine University"
2022
Photograph
Artist Kennedy Miedema
Photo Credit Nicole Watson
Courtesy Jaime Black-Morsette

Page xx–1
"Woman wearing red dress on fire"
© Brandy Bloxom

Page 4
Resilience
2017
Photograph
Artist Jaime Black-Morsette
Photo Credit Jaime Black-Morsette

Page 6–7
"The REDress Project"
2014
Photograph
Artist Jaime Black-Morsette
Photo Credit Sheila Spence

Page 10
"The REDress Project at Kamloops Indian Residential School site"
2011
Photograph
Photo Credit Jaime Black-Morsette

Page 12
"Red jingle dress"
Photograph
© Patrick Chondon Photography

Page 20–21
they tried to bury us
2017
Performance still
Artist Jaime Black-Morsette
Photo Credit M Mousseau

Page 26–27
"Red dress in snow"
Photograph
© Amanda Bracken

Page 29
Honouring Our Spirits in a Good Way
2023
Photograph
© Judith Gale

Page 30
"Family and supporters paint a red dress"
2023
Photograph
© The Canadian Press/John Woods

Page 33
Search the landfill
2023
Photograph
Featuring Grandma Shingoose
Photo Credit Jaime Black-Morsette

Page 34
"We are human, not trash"
2023
Photograph
© Miles Morrisseau/ICT

Page 58–59
"Red dresses in front of a sign reading 'RECONCILIATION'"
Photograph
© Amber Bracken

Page 63
trace
2023
Performance still
Artist Jaime Black-Morsette
Photo Credit NK

Page 64
"Red Dress protest World Police and Fire Games"
2023
Photograph
© Michael Yellowwing Kannon
Photographer's Note: We are the Land. We are the Land that rises up to Defend the Sacred.

Page 75
Walking With Our Sisters
2014
Photograph of installation at the Parry Sound District Museum
© Christi Belcourt

Page 79
Nikâwiy Nitânis
2017
Painting
© Mackenzie Anderson Linklater

Page 80
Audrey Siegl
2019
Scan of 8 x 10 Tintype
© Kali Spitzer

Page 81
The Sound of Healing
2019
Scan of 8 x 10 Tintype
© Kali Spitzer

Page 86
It's Not Your Fault
2015
Video still
© Raven Davis

Page 87
It's Not Your Fault
2015
Video still
© Raven Davis

Page 90
Gone But Not Forgotten
2017
Photograph of installation
Photo Credit Scott Benesiinaabandan
© Casey Koyczan

Page 96
Save Her (Savior)
2020
Mixed media, acrylic paint, photo print, paper, and beadwork on canvas
Featuring Pamela Lepscier
© Crystal Lepscier

Page 106–107
She Holds Water
2018
Photograph
Featuring Jaime Black-Morsette and KC Adams
Photo Credit Lindsay Bond

Page 110
the water in me, recognizes you
2022
Performance still
Artist Jaime Black-Morsette
Photo Credit NK

Page 112
"Eagle staff with feather and red strips of cloth"
Photograph
© Jeannie Whitebird

Page 113
the water in me, recognizes you
2020
Performance still
Artist Jaime Black-Morsette
Photo Credit NK

Page 118–119
"red dress, clay and copper bowl in the lake"
2020
Performance still
Artist Jaime Black-Morsette
Photo Credit NK

Page 127
"Whiteshell Turtle Constellation Petroform"
Photograph
© Diane Maytwayashing/Whiteshell Petroforms

Page 130
"Reconciliation"
2020
Photograph
© Amanda Follett Hosgood

Page 132
skywoman
2021
Photograph
Artist Jaime Black-Morsette
Photo Credit NK

Contributor Biographies

JAIME BLACK-MORSETTE (she/they) is a Red River Métis artist and activist, with family scrip signed in the community of St. Andrews, Manitoba. Jaime lives and works on her home territory near the confluence of the Red and Assiniboine Rivers. Founder of the REDress Project in 2010, Black-Morsette has been using their art practice as a way to gather community and create action and change around the epidemic of violence against Indigenous women, girls, and Two-Spirit people across Turtle Island for over a decade. Black-Morsette's interdisciplinary art practice includes immersive film and video, installation art, photography, and performance art practices. Her work explores themes of memory, identity, place, and resistance.

KC ADAMS (Ininnew/Anishinaabe/British) (she/her) is a registered Fisher River Cree Nation member living in Winnipeg. KC is a relational maker, educator, activist, and mentor who creates work that explores technology in relation to her Indigenous culture. Adams is an award-winning, nationally and internationally known maker with a B.F.A. from Concordia University and an M.A. in Cultural Studies, Curatorial Stream from the University of Winnipeg. KC has had numerous solo and group exhibitions, residencies, and three biennales.

PATTI BEARDY is an Anishinaabe Knowledge Keeper from Lake St. Martin First Nation in Manitoba.

CHRISTI BELCOURT (she/her) is a Métis visual artist, author, and social justice advocate who descends from the Métis community manitow sâkahikan (Lac Ste. Anne), Alberta. In 2012, Christi, along with a national collective, organized Walking With Our Sisters, a ten-year national commemorative installation consisting of over 2,000 pairs of beaded moccasin tops, each pair representing a missing or murdered Indigenous woman or girl. Christi is the recipient of numerous awards and has authored three books. Her artwork can be found in the permanent collections of many galleries, including the National Gallery of Canada, Art Gallery of Ontario, Minneapolis Art Institute, the Gabriel Dumont Institute, and more.

JUDY DA SILVA is an Elder, award-winning activist, and community leader in Grassy Narrows First Nation. She became an advocate for Indigenous rights and environmental justice after a chemical plant dumped 9,000 kilograms of mercury into the river near her community, poisoning the people of Grassy Narrows in the 1960s and 70s. She was awarded the Michael Sattler Peace Prize from the German Mennonite Peace Committee in 2013, and the Extraordinary International Activist award from Human Rights Watch in 2017.

KARINE R. DUHAMEL (she/her/hers) is Anishinaabe and of mixed European heritage, and an off-reserve member of Red Rock First Nation. From 2018 to 2019, Karine was Director of Research for the historic National Inquiry into Missing and Murdered Indigenous Women and Girls, drafting the Final Report, directing the Legacy Archive, and managing the Forensic Document Review Project. In 2020 and 2021, she chaired the Data Sub-Working group that created the MMIWG National Action Plan Data Strategy. She is now Director, Indigenous Strategy for the Social Sciences and Humanities Research Council of Canada.

DEANTHA EDMUNDS (she/her/hers) is Canada's first Inuk professional classical singer. She was appointed a Member of the Order of Canada in December 2023 for her activity as a performer, writer, composer, and mentor—work which seeks to empower Indigenous people and share their stories. Deantha shares her voice and vision with her whole heart, drawing accolades from across Canada and the world.

CAMBRIA HARRIS, WEST FLYING SPARROW WOMAN, lives in Winnipeg, Manitoba, and is a member of the Long Plain First Nation. Cambria is one of the leading voices of the Search The Landfill Movement in response to the Province of Manitoba's refusal to search for her mother's remains in a local landfill. Cambria uses her voice to call for government action and fight for justice for not only her mother but all those affected by MMIWG2S.

JAIMIE ISAAC (she/her/hers) is a curator and interdisciplinary artist, Anishinaabe member of Sagkeeng First Nation, and of British heritage. She was the Chief Curator at the Art Gallery of Greater Victoria from 2021-2023, and advisor 2023-2024. She served as the Curator of Contemporary and Indigenous Arts at the Winnipeg Art Gallery 2015-2021. Isaac holds a degree in Art History from University of Winnipeg and a Masters of Arts from the University of British Columbia focused on decolonizing gallery/museum practices.

CASEY KOYCZAN (he/him/his) is a Dene interdisciplinary artist from Yellowknife, NT, who uses various mediums to communicate how culture and technology can grow together in order for us to develop a better understanding of who we are, where we come from, and where we are going. He creates with whatever tools necessary to bring an idea to fruition, and specializes in sculpture, installation, 3D/VR/AR/360, video, and audio works such as music, soundscapes, and film scores.

CRYSTAL LEPSCIER (WAQSEPĀĒHKETUKIW) (she/her/hers) is an enrolled member of the Little Shell Tribe of Chippewa and a direct descendant of Menominee and Stockbridge-Munsee tribes. She has earned an EdD in First Nations from UW-Green Bay and both her Master of Science degree in Educational Leadership and Policy Analysis (2011) and her Bachelor of Fine Arts in Studio Art (2005) from UW-Madison. Crystal continues to practice traditional and contemporary cultural art forms informed by her tribal communities.

MACKENZIE ANDERSON LINKLATER (she/her/hers) is an artist who creates with beading, printmaking, and installation. She received a Bachelor of Fine Arts degree with Honours at the School of Art at the University of Manitoba. Mackenzie is first degree Midewiwin at the Minweyweygan Lodge in Roseau River First Nation and her true name is Mispon Kisikaw Iskwew or Goonagiizhagokwe, which translates to Snowy Sky Woman.

LEE-ANN MARTIN (she/her/hers) is an independent curator of Indigenous Art. Previously she was the Head Curator at the MacKenzie Art Gallery in Regina, Saskatchewan, and Curator of Contemporary Canadian Aboriginal Art at the Canadian Museum of Civilization in Gatineau, Quebec. Martin was the recipient of the Governor General's Award in Visual and Media Arts (2019) and received an Honorary Doctorate from Concordia University in 2022.

DIANE MAYTWAYASHING (she/her/Ikwe) is an Anishinaabekwe, mother, grandmother, and great-grandmother. Her family heritage originates from Lake Manitoba, and today she lives in Seven Sisters Falls, Manitoba, near Whiteshell Provincial Park. Diane is a land-based educator on Indigenous people of the Whiteshell and heritage interpreter of the sacred stone formations (petroforms) in Whiteshell Park. She is a women's pipe carrier, veteran sun dancer, teacher of Indigenous Matrilineal societies, and conductor of many ceremonies.

CATHY MERRICK (1962–2024) was a proud Cree woman from the Cross Lake Band of Indians in northern Manitoba. Merrick's leadership journey began as a Councillor in Pimicikamak, where she served for twelve years. After forty-four years of male leadership, Merrick was the second woman to be elected as Chief of Pimicikamak in 2013 and remained Chief for an impactful five years as per Pimicikamak election law. In October 2022, she made history by becoming the first female Grand Chief elected to the Assembly of Manitoba Chiefs.

SHERRY FARRELL RACETTE (Métis/Algonquin/Irish) (she/her/hers) is an interdisciplinary scholar with an active arts and curatorial practice. She has worked extensively in archives and museum collections with an emphasis on retrieving women's voices and recovering knowledge. Currently teaching in the Faculty of Media, Art, and Performance (art history), she was previously cross-appointed to the Departments of Native Studies and Women's and Gender Studies at the University of Manitoba, and the Department of Art History at Concordia University, Montreal. In 2021 she received a Lifetime Achievement Award from the University Art Association of Canada.

GLADYS RADEK (she/her/hers) is a human rights activist originally from the Gitxsan Wet'suwet'en territory in northern British Columbia, known as the Highway of Tears. In response to the disappearance of her niece in 2005, Gladys co-founded the grassroots organization Walk4Justice in 2008 to bring the families affected by MMIWG together. Today, she continues to raise awareness by placing pictures of MMIWG on her van and supports healing for family members and youth through her work as an Elder for her sister's organization, the Tears to Hope Society.

ZOEY ROY (she/her/hers) is an award-winning Cree-Dene Halfbreed Métis spoken word poet and teaching artist. She operates a creative consulting company out of Ottawa, Ontario, and is a PhD student at York University, focusing on songwriting as future-building. Zoey has received the Queen's Diamond Jubilee Medal, the Women of Distinction Award in Saskatoon, Saskatchewan, and the Indspire Award, and she was most recently recognized as the University of Saskatchewan's One to Watch.

JENNIFER LEE SMITH (she/her/hers) is a Red River Métis curator, writer, and arts administrator living on Treaty 1 Territory/Winnipeg. Her work focuses on the relationships between Indigenous artists, connections to land and material culture.